The Encouraging Parent

The
Encouraging Parent

How to stop *Yelling at Your Kids*

and start *Teaching Them*

Confidence, Self-Discipline, and Joy

ROD WALLACE KENNEDY, Ph.D.

THREE RIVERS PRESS • NEW YORK

Grateful acknowledgment is made to the following for permission to reprint previously published material:

HarperCollins Publishers: Excerpt from *The Art of Loving* by Erich Fromm. Copyright © 1956 by Erich Fromm. Reprinted by permission of HarperCollins Publishers.

HarperCollins Publishers and Broken Moon Press: Excerpt from *Little Altars Everywhere* by Rebecca Wells. Copyright © 1992 by Rebecca Wells. Originally published by Broken Moon Press. Excerpted by permission of Broken Moon Press and HarperCollins Publishers.

Alfred A. Knopf: Excerpts from *Oldest Living Confederate Widow Tells All* by Allan Gurganas. Copyright © 1989 by Allan Gurganas. Reprinted by permission of Alfred A. Knopf, a division of Random House, Inc.

Lindamichellebaron: Stanza from "Once Upon a Time" by Lindamichellebaron. © Lindamichellebaron, Ed.D.

Published by Three Rivers Press, New York, New York.
Member of the Crown Publishing Group.

Random House, Inc. New York, Toronto, London, Sydney, Auckland
www.randomhouse.com

THREE RIVERS PRESS is a registered trademark and the Three Rivers Press colophon is a trademark of Random House, Inc.

Printed in the United States of America

Designed by LEONARD HENDERSON

Library of Congress Cataloging-in-Publication Data

Kennedy, Rodney.
　　The encouraging parent: how to stop yelling at your kids and start teaching them confidence, self-discipline, and joy / Rodney Wallace Kennedy.— 1st ed.
　　　　p. cm.
　　1. Child rearing. 2. Parenting. 3. Parent and child. 4. Discipline of children. 5. Self-control in children. I. Title.
HQ769.K375 2001
649'.1—dc21

　　　　　　　　　　　　　　　　　　　　　　　　　　　00-056770

ISBN 0-8129-3313-3 (pbk.)
10　9　8　7　6　5　4　3

Dedicated to
Johnelle Wallace Kennedy,
the model of encouragement

CONTENTS

ACKNOWLEDGMENTS

WHILE THIS BOOK IS a remembrance of many years as a parent and as a teacher of parents, I am indebted to several gifted people in particular who have inspired and encouraged me. Most of all, I would like to thank my partner, friend, encourager, lover, teacher, and spouse, Johnelle, for her incredible insights into the hearts of children. Much of the material in this book has come from Johnelle's parenting greatness as well as her thirty years of experience as a classroom teacher and school principal. Without her, there would have never been a book called *The Encouraging Parent*.

I'd also like to thank our children, Vin, Kirkland, Melissa, Jennifer, and Jeffrey, for their contributions to the book. Their willingness to expose the struggles of growing into adulthood with a wider audience makes this work more biographical than first intended. For all their foibles and misdeeds traced through these pages, I must tell you of the sheer joy and satisfaction they have brought to my life.

There are several gifted friends who have pushed me to complete this work. I would like to thank Ed Boyd, Charles Simmons, and Stacie Schneider for their encouragement and insights. Betsy Rapoport, my editor, "the queen of commas," worked very hard with amazing kindness to turn my sometimes arcane and academic use of language into popular and conversational style. Stephanie Higgs kept me focused on the task at hand and gently reminded me of deadlines around every corner. Wendy Keller, my agent, brought a practical guidance to the business side of the book, and without her help I would never have finished. Finally, I must thank Jeff and Rita Kennedy, my parents. They taught me the meaning of encouragement.

PREFACE

THE PARENT TEST

THE TIME HAS COME to evaluate parents. We hold our schools accountable on the basis of the scores students make on standardized tests. We evaluate our teachers on a whole series of issues. Assessment of students is a big part of educational evaluation. In other words, everyone in the educational equation gets an evaluation except parents. Parents, who so often forget that teachers are their allies and not their adversaries, aren't graded. Are we afraid we'll hurt their feelings? Are today's parents too sensitive to take the pressure of an honest evaluation? The parents attending my workshops would answer no to these questions. They are interested in being the best possible parents.

Over the past four years, I've worked with more than 100,000 parents and teachers. The result of hundreds of workshops and my ongoing research led me to develop The Parent Test, a tool that will help you measure your effectiveness in a number of crucial areas. While this particular evaluation form is self-administered, I have found that parents have a keen interest in their performance. The test contains 50 indicators that will enable you to determine how well you're doing in the following areas: providing discipline, fostering your kids' success, communicating effectively, and having a positive parenting attitude.

This evaluation has been designed in the most nonthreatening way possible. I'll ask you to rate yourself on a sliding scale of 1–5. The lowest possible evaluation is a 1, representing unsatisfactory performance. The highest possible score is a 5, representing outstanding performance. Since there are 50 indicators in the evaluation, the highest possible score is 250. A score below 150 means you need improvement. A score of 150–200: Satisfactory. A score of 201–250: Outstanding.

The purpose of this evaluation is to help you discover where you need to improve as a parent. For example, if you spend little or no time talking with your children and have difficulty expressing your feelings, you'll want to work on improving interpersonal communication skills.

If you have self-control issues such as temper tantrums, screaming and yelling, or abusive language, you'll want to work on conflict management strategies as well as managing anger. I believe that most parents are willing to reflect honestly on their parenting experiences. The majority of parents want to do a good job. They really want to help their children succeed. You are one of those parents. You can learn to be a more encouraging parent.

THE PARENT TEST

Directions: Indicate the appropriate rating of each major topic by circling the 5 (outstanding), 4 (excellent), 3 (above average), 2 (average), or 1 (below average). Total your score when you're done.

Discipline

I am comfortable disciplining my children.	5	4	3	2	1
I have high expectations and goals for my children.	5	4	3	2	1
I allow my children to make as many real choices as possible.	5	4	3	2	1
I have established routines for my children.	5	4	3	2	1
My discipline is more of a game than a battle.	5	4	3	2	1

My discipline is consistent.	5	4	3	2	1
I have a few basic general rules.	5	4	3	2	1
I give my children immediate, natural, and reasonable consequences for misbehavior.	5	4	3	2	1
I have a consistent philosophy of discipline.	5	4	3	2	1
I believe in spanking.	5	4	3	2	1
I use rewards to motivate my children's behavior.	5	4	3	2	1

Academic Success

I read to my child at least three times a week during the first five years of his/her life.	5	4	3	2	1
I help my child with homework.	5	4	3	2	1
I expect my child to make good grades.	5	4	3	2	1
I attend open house at the beginning of each school year.	5	4	3	2	1
I check my child's homework.	5	4	3	2	1
I ask my child how he/she is doing in school.	5	4	3	2	1
I encourage creativity and imagination in my child.	5	4	3	2	1
I introduce my children to the best literature.	5	4	3	2	1
I meet with my child's teacher to discuss goals and expectations.	5	4	3	2	1
I attend PTA meetings.	5	4	3	2	1
I volunteer at my child's school.	5	4	3	2	1
I attend events at school.	5	4	3	2	1
I teach my child good study skills.	5	4	3	2	1
I help my child learn new skills.	5	4	3	2	1

Communication

I provide consistent emotional support for my children.	5	4	3	2	1
I use the language of high expectancy.	5	4	3	2	1

I am a good listener.	5	4	3	2	1
I am an honest and open person.	5	4	3	2	1
I provide my children regular feedback on their behavior.	5	4	3	2	1
I have excellent rapport with my children.	5	4	3	2	1
I spend at least thirty minutes a day talking with my children.	5	4	3	2	1
I communicate with my children in a variety of ways.	5	4	3	2	1
I tell my children how I feel.	5	4	3	2	1
I tell my children lots of stories.	5	4	3	2	1
I communicate the importance of education.	5	4	3	2	1

Attitude

I have a positive attitude toward parenting.	5	4	3	2	1
I enjoy my children.	5	4	3	2	1
I am a patient parent.	5	4	3	2	1
I do not lose my temper.	5	4	3	2	1
I do not scream at my children.	5	4	3	2	1
I treat my children with dignity and respect.	5	4	3	2	1
I am a calm parent.	5	4	3	2	1
I practice self-control and self-discipline.	5	4	3	2	1
I believe my kids can do well.	5	4	3	2	1
I model empathy, caring, and helpfulness.	5	4	3	2	1
My conversation and my conduct are the same.	5	4	3	2	1
My children can't get me to lose my cool.	5	4	3	2	1
I don't use sarcasm and putdowns.	5	4	3	2	1
I don't use abusive language.	5	4	3	2	1

TOTAL SCORE _____

The Encouraging Parent

CHAPTER 1

BECOMING THE ENCOURAGER

WELCOME TO *THE ENCOURAGING PARENT*—a book designed to encourage parents in every kind of family. I want to help you become better parents. And I'm in a position to help because my five children have reached the state of blessedness—*they're grown and gone.* Encouragement is the most basic parenting inclination. We start out as encouragers. To encourage means to build up, to seek good, to put courage in a child's heart, to be positive, to motivate, to persuade, to inspire, to enlighten, and to help. Because I seek to be an "encourager" in the lives of my children, I think of my parenting in personal, relationship-building ways. Parents today don't need more guilt or stress. They need strength. With encouragement, we can build hope in the hearts of our children. Parents need to know that encouragement has far more potential to help develop emotionally healthy children than punitive measures like spanking.

Each year I speak to more than 30,000 parents. They share their dreams and their frustrations with me. I do 150 to 200 workshops for parents every year all across the United States. What I have learned from thousands of interviews, conversations, question and answer sessions, and surveys is that there is no "typical" American family. But behind the different kinds of families there remains the parental longing to raise children in safety, security, and wholeness. I spend the majority of my time helping parents solve the very real and practical problems of raising children. My academic background is in communication and I have a Ph.D. in speech communication. *The Encouraging Parent* is designed to combine the communication theory I've learned and researched in the anecdotal experiences of parenting drawn from my own family and what I've learned from families in my workshops.

AN EXPANDED DEFINITION OF FAMILY

There is no one particular definition of family that every family has to fit. While proponents of "the traditional family" insist that there is only one acceptable way to raise children, I don't concur. In my experience as the parent of five children it isn't whether Mom stays home with them or works that's the deciding factor. What matter are the quality and consistency of care that our children receive. Contemporary families often bear little resemblance to traditional definitions. There are a variety of viable family paradigms in our culture. The world has changed and the family paradigm of the 1940s has shifted. Single parents and dual-career families aren't going to suddenly disappear. After all, the mom-at-home model is an isolated trend in parenting, not the historical norm.

We need a broader and more acceptable definition of family—a definition that doesn't imply guilt and shame for people living in nontraditional families. I will define family as an organized group of people living together, sharing together, and building relationships together over an extended period of time. Whether your family is a "traditional family" or not has little bearing on the matter. I have written this book to encourage single parents, dual-career parents, divorced parents, stepfamily parents, and grandparents raising their grandchildren. It's how you parent, not the composition of your family, that counts.

A WORD OF ENCOURAGEMENT FOR
NONTRADITIONAL FAMILIES

While a number of parenting experts insist that Mom stay home with the children, this isn't necessarily right for everyone. The appeal to religious authority in this matter doesn't prove that women have to stay home rather than engage in meaningful careers. The options are multiple.

The issue is one of personal choice, not particular mandate. Parenting is hard enough and exhausting enough without the attempts of sincere, well-meaning people heaping more guilt on dual-career families. I dissent from the popular view that families do best with a stay-at-home mom. Recent research indicates that working moms spend as much time with their children as stay-at-home moms did in the 1950s. Mom can stay home if she really wants to, and I have no problem with her decision. But Mom can also have a career and children and that can be just as good a decision for her and for the family.

Many of the critics of our culture lay all the blame on the family. They cry for the "good old days" when the family was made up of a man and his wife and three children. But were the good old days ever that good? Was the family ever free of violence? In *The Care of the Soul,* Thomas Moore writes, "Many people who come to therapy today were raised in the so-called golden age of the family, and yet they tell stories of abuse, neglect, and terrifying moralistic demands and pressures. Looked at coldly, the family of any era is both good and bad, offering both support and threat." Painful memories and difficult relationships are the stuff of family life.

Moore continues, "Today professionals are preoccupied with the 'dysfunctional family.' But to some extent all families are dysfunctional. No family is perfect, and most have serious problems. A family is a microcosm, reflecting the nature of the world, which runs on both virtue and evil. We may be tempted at times to imagine the family as full of innocence and good will, but actual family life resists such romanticism. Any attempts to place a veil of simplistic sentimentality over the family image will break down."

We can't go back. No matter how sincere the prophets of restoration of the traditional family are, no matter how deeply the preachers of "the good old days" may believe, we can't go back. Nothing is more suitable for the care of the soul than family. According to Shirley Steinberg and Joe Kincheloe in *Kinderculture,* "Advocates of traditional family values and severe discipline for children understand that something has changed, that for some reason authority has broken down. Such advocates often attribute the breakdown of authority to feminism and its encouragement of mothers to pursue careers outside of the home and to permissive liberals who opposed corporal punishment and other harsh forms of child control. Unfortunately for the welfare of children, they're wrong. Adult authority over children, no doubt, has broken down, but not because of feminist mothers or wimpy liberals. Children's access to the adult world via the electronic media of hyperreality has subverted contemporary children's consciousness of themselves as incompetent and dependent entities. Such a self-perception doesn't mix well with institutions such as the traditional family or the authoritarian school, institutions both grounded on a view of children as incapable of making decisions for themselves."

To live in a family is to experience all the complexity of human life. There are too many simplistic understandings of what it means to live in a good, functional, and happy family. There is good and bad in all families. We need less judgment and less pressure. Since there is no ideal family, we can learn to embrace the family that's ours. We can learn to be at peace with the shadows and the stories that make up each individual family.

For every single parent and working mom who has internalized the blame and guilt and shame propagated by the traditional family proponents, I offer encouragement. The issue that really matters is for your children to have an intimate, affectionate environment and a loving, positive relationship with you.

For me, raising children is an exercise in controlled insanity. It's not necessary to be great scholar or child psychologist to see that many families today aren't in good health. Each year as I speak to parents, I hear stories of anxiety, stress, pain, and brokenness. Family ills are innumerable; they exist in an odd mixture of pleasure and pain. What can we do to help?

Many parenting experts have attempted a diagnosis. Some of them have done so with a certainty, an air of authority, that disturbs me. I'm convinced that the reductionistic appeal to return to the golden age of family life is a myth. The ever-expanding library of parenting books convinces me that there is no one perfect approach to raising children. Everyone who writes about parenting as well as every adult practicing the art of parenting is searching for answers.

RELATIONSHIPS AND COMMUNICATION

What matters is the nature of the relationships that you form with your children. Relationships are complex and multiple in nature. They include individual family members, the ways they interact with each other, treat each other, communicate with each other, and connect with the overall family. The actual makeup of the family isn't nearly as important as the relationships that are being built day by day.

There are no easy paths to building relationships, but I believe that we all have the ability to be good parents and build good, strong relationships with our children. The crucial component in building relationships is communication: sharing our thoughts with one another. All family members contribute to the ongoing series of conversations that make up the family. Whenever a new baby comes home from the hospital, he or she joins a family conversation that has been going on forever. In fact, each member of the family joins the conversation from another conversation in their family of origin. The original conversation echoes throughout the new conversation that's being constructed each day by the members of the family. There is a constant give-and-take. The family thus functions better as a democracy than as dictatorship. Together families communicate to increase understanding and develop common ground or rapport.

HOSPITALITY

An essential element of communication in families is *hospitality*. I define hospitality as making a space in our souls for the other members of the family. This is a welcoming space. In other words, it's a place we construct so that other members of the family know they're accepted and welcomed and loved.

All families develop a style of relating through sending and receiving multiple messages whose meanings develop over time. This includes verbal and nonverbal messages. Images, metaphors, stories, actions, and words coalesce to produce meaning for parents and children. In other words, our talking and our acting builds our families over time.

THE FRUSTRATIONS OF PARENTING

The parents attending my workshops frequently reveal a deep anxiety. While some may pretend to be sure of themselves, they're hiding nervousness and stress. They confess a sense of dissatisfaction and frustration with their attempts at being good parents. Usually the honest admission of fear and anxiety is the first step in becoming a better parent. After all, it's a scary thing to raise children in our time.

A second frustration that parents reveal is that their efforts don't produce the results they expect. Part of the reason for the frustration is impatience. Parents expect too much too soon.

A third frustration is that the very efforts they make to be effective parents often make them even more ineffective. When they try to communicate with their children and create an atmosphere of understanding, they often go about it in a way that multiplies the misunderstandings. They work at parenting with such desperation that they lose all sense of self-control and are more confused than ever.

The parents in my workshops tell me that the parenting books they read make them feel more frustrated than before. "They make it sound so easy." "That author never had a son like mine." "I can't think up all these clever, creative ways of disciplining my daughter." Putting theory into practice is never easy. Parenting books often fail to deal adequately with the mess that families are in. They don't accept the reality of families with negative climates and poisoned atmospheres. They don't realize how many parents continue to carry on like their parents before them. One editor, reviewing my material, said, "I don't believe that many parents actually scream at their children." That's not what parents tell me: "I don't mean to yell. The kids just get on my nerves." "I know I shouldn't scream, but I just don't know what else to do." "Kids drive me nuts. They don't listen. They ignore me. So I yell and scream all the time." "You have to get their attention." "I'm a screamer, but I want to stop. Can you help me?"

I'm not writing this book to convince you that I'm the parenting expert you've been waiting for—although I do have some helpful advice I intend to pass along. I'm writing to convince you that you are already the parenting expert in your home. No one knows your kids more and loves them better. You just need to ditch what you're doing that isn't working and go back to being the born encourager you are. I'll show you how.

THE PARENTING STRUGGLE

How are things at home? I want to know how life is going with you and your children. Who's really in charge? You or your children? Tell the truth. Some parents—I facetiously refer to them as "permissive possum parents"—allow their children to be in charge. A possum is an animal that pretends to be dead when confronted by danger, thus the old saying, "She's playing possum." Possum parents are too busy, too distracted, and too softhearted to be in charge. Does that description fit your approach to parenting? Or do you belong at the opposite end of the spectrum and run your family like a boot camp? You're in charge and everyone knows it. No one would dare buck you or refuse one of your dictatorial demands.

Some parents think they're in charge, when, in fact, the children are calling the shots. Well, I have good news for you. As a parent, you *should* be in charge. That's what it means to be a parent. However, you can be in charge without being mean, rude, obnoxious, or overbearing. You can be in charge without losing your temper and threatening to beat your kids. You can be a great parent without spanking your kids.

PARENTS NEED A POSITIVE APPROACH

The punitive approach has the solid support of a sizable portion of the religious community. A national workshop, Growing Kids God's Way, is an example of the direct support that punitive measures, such as spanking, receive in our culture. The very title of the workshop strikes me as presumptuous. How can anyone actually claim to know God's way of raising children? Many parenting manuals tout the validity of spanking. Sure, they've toned down the punitive nature of their rhetoric. They make spanking sound like a benevolent act on the part of parents—"I'm spanking you for your own good."

Throughout this book, I will insist that spanking is an unnecessary discipline technique whose time has come and gone. Simply put, *"Stop the spanking."* In parenting workshops across the country, I struggle to convince parents that spanking is never necessary. In a recent workshop in North Carolina, an obviously sincere dad asked me incredulously how he could possibly discipline a sixteen-month-old child without spanking her. He was not a mean or incorrigible person. He wanted to do the right thing. Yet the idea of discipline without spanking confused him.

In my interviews with parents, I've been surprised by the prevalent feelings about traditional, hard-nosed, punitive measures. One dad said, for example, "This is a waste of time. I don't need some expert telling me how to raise my kids. When kids get out of line, all you have to do is beat the hell out of them. They'll straighten up and fly right." Fiction writers often describe in graphic detail how this punitive approach to parenting affected their lives, reflecting it in the lives of their characters. While the material may be categorized as fictional, the words are often autobiographical: "It was rough as a cob back then." "That boy needs somebody to take a belt to his ass." "There's nothing wrong with children today that a belt wouldn't cure."

Part of the reason for the deep entrenchment of the philosophy of spanking has to do with the religious support of the practice. This isn't a religious book for parents, but I do feel that we need to look closely at the religious reasons often cited in support of spanking, which I'll do in the next chapter. If these reasons turn out to be more rooted in cultural prejudice than in any "word of God," then we will be freer to reject spanking as an acceptable discipline for children.

I believe that spanking is the final vestige of a patriarchal culture that provided men with unparalleled superiority and control. Not too long ago in the evolving relationship between men and women, men were not held accountable for abusing their wives. In many areas, wife beating was an acceptable practice. So for centuries men beat their wives, their children, and their animals. Today, no husband in his right mind would advocate his right to hit his wife. Yet parenting experts, especially religious ones, continue to insist that spanking isn't only right, but that God ordains that parents should spank their children. I disagree. You won't find any positive apology for spanking in these pages.

Some parents remind me with righteous assurance that the Bible commands spanking as a practical necessity. The verse of Scripture that's most frequently quoted is Proverbs 13:24. "Spare the rod and spoil the child" is the banner under which spanking proponents have marched across the centuries. Parents are left with the reductionistic choice of spanking or spoiling.

With as much care as possible, I dissent with this view for a number of reasons. First, the aphorism from Proverbs is one of hundreds. Many of these sayings are the direct result of ancient culture and don't carry the weight of divine authority. For example, seven times the writer or writers of Proverbs use the following statement: "It's better for a man to live on a corner of the rooftop than in the house with a nagging wife." No one ever quotes *that* sexist text! I'm not convinced that one proof text from the Bible gives parents the right to hit their children.

I want to suggest that parents can be in charge and be strong disciplinarians without ever spanking their children. Spanking is unnecessary, barbaric, and a misuse of parental power. I want to affirm that you're in charge, but I want to show you how to be in charge without hitting your children.

We can teach our children how to be in charge of their own behavior. Let's give our children two gifts: self-control and self-discipline. Let's raise children today the same way we've always raised good children—with fair, enforceable rules and consistent consequences. Make sure that you fashion rules and consequences with love, maturity, and tenderness. In other words, be firm and fair. Be tough and tender.

We've raised a whole generation on the gospel of self-esteem. Today's kids have bushel baskets of self-esteem, but it hasn't been enough. Self-esteem is only a partial truth. In part to blame is the misguided self-esteem movement that permeates nearly all our parenting philosophies. But self-worth, as opposed to self-esteem, isn't bestowed. It's earned through the products of the hardest work out there: self-control. Feeling good about yourself is the result of doing well.

How do we raise children of worth? Self-control is the greatest gift parents can impart to their children.

Children tend to adopt the attitudes of their parents toward life.

Recent research indicates that while children are most affected by their peers when it comes to behavior, they're more likely to think like their parents when it comes to attitudes toward sex, race, and religion. Our attitudes generally become that of our children. That means our attitudes are crucial to their development. That's why self-control and self-discipline are the most important ingredients in the parenting experience. If we're resilient, we bounce back from adversity; if we're pessimistic, we're overwhelmed by problems.

When a pessimistic parent makes a mistake, it has to be someone else's fault. Even small mistakes are magnified into personal disasters with lasting results. Before long, children learn to make excuses and to place blame for everything that happens: "It's not my fault. Mother didn't give me my medicine." "I'm late because Dad couldn't find his keys." "He made me hit him."

Other parents see everything that occurs as insignificant. Whatever happens is somehow OK: "I'm always sloppy. I can't ever keep the house clean." "I'm always late. It runs in the family." "I can't control my temper. I'm just like my daddy."

Children grow up listening to a plethora of mistakes and excuses. That leads to whining, crying, and blaming others. No one in the family admits to mistakes, and no one takes responsibility. The problems in the family are never resolved and are therefore repeated over and over. The stress level in the home goes through the roof. Parents repeat the same ineffective techniques of discipline day after day.

Problems and mistakes and difficulty and adversity overwhelm many parents because they've got such a pessimistic attitude or world view. Problem-solving is a better approach. This book will show you the basis of conflict resolution and how to teach kids to get along with each other. It'll also show you how to keep your cool.

Parenting has a lot to do with our ability to maintain self-control.

A seventh grade student in my wife's school had a bad habit of losing his temper and hitting other students. One day, as he was sitting in Johnelle's office, she asked him, "Why did you hit Jerome?" He replied, "I couldn't help myself. He made me hit him."

He expected his defense to work because he'd been using it most of his life. His parents had long ago given up and embraced the philosophy: "You know how John is. When he gets mad, stay out of his way." I'm sure he was surprised when Johnelle insisted that he was responsible for his temper and his anger and his actions. "I think," she told John, "that you need to think about your behavior and then figure out what you're going to do the next time you get angry. The basic fact is that other people can't *make* you angry or *make* you hit others. Kids may tease you, provoke you, or intimidate you, but *whether you get angry or not is entirely your choice.* You alone are responsible for that choice and for accepting the consequences that come with it."

In interviews with thousands of parents, I have learned that parents often feel desperate, out of control, and guilty from the practice of old-fashioned discipline techniques. Out of frustration, they often resort to spanking and coercion. The result of all this confusion is a cycle of misbehavior, blame, punishment, and guilt. The cycle is repeated on an almost daily basis. I want to help parents break the destructive cycle of punishment.

My aim is to show you how to become encouragers, empowering you to teach your children a way of life that prepares them for maturity. Unlike other books on parenting, *The Encouraging Parent* doesn't prescribe quick fixes or superficial approaches with treats, bribes, spankings, or charts. Instead I will outline an approach to parenting that includes teaching, mentoring, creating routines, problem-solving, instilling responsibility, and building relationships. Discipline will be treated as a minor key in the marvelous symphony that's parenting. I will encourage you to create your own unique plan for raising your children by employing encouraging principles in combination with such parenting roles as teacher, mentor, coach, and manager.

A POSITIVE WORD FOR PARENTS

As a parent, you already possess the necessary knowledge and skill to do a great job of raising your children. You may need more confidence, more patience, and more self-control, but you already know how to parent. The following simple vignette encompasses the heart of my message:

Three-year-old Jason asks his mom for a bar of candy at Albertson's Supermarket. Mom smiles and says, "No." Jason has a typical allergic reaction to the word *no*. He falls down on the floor and throws a temper tantrum.

Mom's first reaction is to glance anxiously around the store. She's checking to see if any of her neighbors are watching. Why? She's worrying about what people will think. Well, let me clear that moment of anxiety for all parents. When other adults see your child having a temper tantrum in the supermarket, they all have the same thought: "Thank God that's not my child." That's not so bad, is it? You can safely deal with your child's outrageous behavior content in the knowledge that all other parents have empathy for you. We're so happy it's you and not us "standing in need of help."

Jason's mom surveys the emotional damage spilling all over the soft drink aisle and considers her options. That's a good move. Parents can take their time dealing with misbehavior. After all, you have all the time in the world and you're in charge. So Mom takes a deep breath and says, "I can handle this." With confidence and calmness, she allows her child to continue his outpouring of protest.

Then she leans into the chaos that is a flailing, screaming three-year-old and quietly asks Jason to be quiet. His response, of course, is to scream louder and kick faster. "You're the meanest mother. I want my candy." She ignores the tantrum, finishes her shopping, and takes Jason home. As soon as she gets home, she leaves all the groceries in the car, and takes Jason inside and disciplines him by sending him to his room and calmly reminding him that he can't have any candy today.

If Jason's mom had been taking a parenting examination, she would have passed with flying colors. Under immense pressure, she decided to eliminate a number of negative options. She didn't scream at Jason, threaten him, beat him, or bribe him. She chose to ride out the storm, ignore the looks from other shoppers, and deal with her son at home. She's in charge of herself, her feelings, her emotions, and her choices. Her emotional maturity is of greater impact than the discipline she decides to use with Jason. With time and repeated lessons, Jason will learn to model his mom's calm self-control.

THE ENCOURAGER

My wife, Johnelle, has always been my personal model for the encouraging parent. She's the definition of encouragement. Not only has she served as encourager to our children, but also for the hundreds of children she has taught in elementary school. Now she shares her gift of encouragement with the 580 students of Glasgow Middle School in Baton Rouge, Louisiana.

One year she had a challenging student named Lawrence in her third-grade class at Goodwood Elementary School. Lawrence, on a good day, was a difficult assignment. Johnelle, in her determined way, refused to give up on Lawrence. She tried everything to unlock the anger in this particular eight-year-old boy. Nothing worked. Lawrence continued to disrupt the class and misbehave. One day, while grading a basic math skills test that her class had taken, Johnelle noticed that Lawrence had scored the highest possible grade. She walked over to Lawrence and told him, "Lawrence, you're so good in math. You would make a great banker." Lawrence smiled for the first time that semester.

The next day I dropped by to have lunch with Johnelle and her class. I find this a wonderful way to demonstrate my undying love and loyalty to my wife. After all, lunch in the school cafeteria with over 150 elementary students isn't exactly what I would consider a romantic outing. Lawrence came running over to me. "Mr. Kennedy! Mrs. Kennedy says I can be a banker. Do you believe her?" "Yes," I said. "If Mrs. Kennedy says you can be a banker, then you can be president of Citibank!" Lawrence beamed with pride.

The next day, however, Lawrence came back to school in a sullen mood. He was up to his old tricks of misbehavior. Johnelle walked over to his desk and stood there silently. Lawrence ignored her. She then touched him on the shoulder and indicated her disapproval of the misbehavior by shaking her head. Lawrence again ignored the nonverbal message. She then asked Lawrence to have a seat at the desk next to hers at the back of the room. During this time she continued teaching her class so that Lawrence didn't get the impression that he was in charge.

After a few minutes, she gave the class a writing assignment, and walked back to talk with Lawrence. "What's the problem? Why are you so angry?" she asked. Lawrence responded, "My mama says you're crazy. I can't be a banker. She says I'm never going to be good for anything but cutting other people's grass." Lawrence, facing that kind of put-down, didn't appear to have much going for him. I'm sure his mom didn't mean her harsh assessment of Lawrence. Probably she was exhausted and the words just slipped out of her mouth.

Two months later, the guidance counselor came to Johnelle's class for an activity called "The Good Friend Award." Each child was asked to select a partner. Then the guidance counselor passed out a certificate for each child to fill out and present to his or her partner. The certificate read, "I give this Good Friend Award to _____ because _____ _____." The purpose of the exercise was for each child to have a positive reason for being a good friend.

Lawrence refused to participate, so Johnelle became his partner. Finally, Lawrence scribbled some words on his certificate. When he presented his Good Friend Award to Johnelle, he read the following words: "I give this Good Friend Award to Mrs. Kennedy because she loves me and wants me to be a banker."

Do you see why I'm such a believer in encouragement? Adults have such awesome power to influence children in positive ways through the words of encouragement. I ask you to find ways to encourage your children with positive words.

In the Walt Disney film *The Lion King,* there's a powerful scene where the baby lion is held up by the jungle prophet and shown to the entire animal kingdom. The song of sheer joy that erupts from the animals is a metaphor for the way all adults should encourage children. The important lesson is that encouragement is a powerful and positive motivator for children.

There are plenty of kids like Lawrence in our world. There is never a time when a child deserves to be put down or embarrassed or humiliated by an adult. That's emotional battering and abuse. When children are subjected to constant criticism and put-downs, they begin to see themselves as not good enough. Children have the right not to hear emotional verbal abuse. Life requires encouragement. Parents need to create safe, respectful, secure, warm places where children know they're loved, cared for, accepted, appreciated, and encouraged.

ENCOURAGE WITHOUT FEAR

Whenever I talk to parents at parenting workshops, I begin by telling them not to be afraid of their children or of the situations they find themselves in while dealing with them. One of the discoveries I have made in talking to parents all over the United States is that many young parents are afraid. Of what? They're afraid if not being good parents, of ruining their children, and afraid their children won't love them if they're firm and in charge. Well, there is no reason for fear. Like the artificial guilt imposed on parents by proponents of the traditional family, fear is a negative emotion that can be overcome.

A harried mom asked me, "Can you help? I'm afraid I'm ruining my children. I find myself sitting in the bed at two in the morning, eating vanilla ice cream and crying, 'I'm ruining my children. I'm ruining my children.'" I told her, "Stop crying. You're not ruining your children. All parents make mistakes because none of us are perfect. Instead of worrying about ruin and despair, I want you to concentrate on the encouraging ways that you can help your children grow."

Our children are growing up in a complex world, and we're often afraid for them. The cultural revolution spawned by the information explosion has changed the world of childhood. Why are so many children strong-willed and defiant? The answer, at least in large part, lies in the fact that children don't see themselves as dependent persons in need of adult permission to operate. They act like mini-adults, and as parents we forget that they are still children in need of our strong guidance. Our task is to help our children make sense of the illusory hyperreality created by the chaos of information. Therefore we cannot allow fear to dictate our approach to raising children.

In the face of his brave new world, a lot of parents and teachers often cry out for "old-fashioned discipline." Parents often say, "Boy, I would have never acted like that as a child. My father would have beaten my behind. That's what we need." The temptation is great, but if we will practice encouragement, we can avoid the choice of fear.

When children sense fear, they rush into the vacuum created by the absence of parental authority and take charge. During a tour of Alabama to do a series of parenting workshops, I stopped at a restaurant in Greenville for the Sunday buffet. There was a long line of people. Behind me in line was a little girl approximately nine years old. Her mom, tired of standing in line, decided she wanted to leave and go to Subway for a quick sandwich. The idea sounded appealing to me as well. Instead of explaining the situation and leaving immediately for Subway, Mom leaned over and asked her daughter, "Would you like to go to Subway for a sandwich or stay here?" The nine-year-old, accustomed to having it her way, stomped her foot, crossed her arms, gave her mother a hateful look, and announced in a public address announcer's voice, "I'm staying right here. I hate Subway." Mom, afraid to be firm, allowed her nine-year-old child to dictate the decision of the entire family. In case you were wondering, the entire family stayed in the long buffet line and had lunch. Unfortunately they were seated at the table right across from me. Mom and daughter had three more confrontations before dessert was served. A child in charge of parents isn't a pretty sight.

I encourage you to take charge and be in charge. Children need parents to be strong without being loud, mean, rude, or harsh.

ENCOURAGEMENT: THE KEY PRINCIPLE

I'm convinced that encouragement is the key parenting principle for the fast-paced world of active, hardworking parents. Parenting on the run is your only option. There is no time to catch your breath. You need answers and you need them now. You need a low-stress approach to parenting. You need real help. Well, encouragement is the key.

I call parenting power E-8th power: Encouragement, Endowment, Enabling, Enlightenment, Empathy, Embellishment, Empowerment, and Emancipation. First we encourage our children to be good people. We endow them with the qualities that will help them grow in this challenge. We enable them to succeed. We enlighten them when they're confused. We show empathy when they're angry or discouraged. We embellish our core lessons with additional skills to speed them along. We empower them to take responsibility for their own behavior. When they're ready, we emancipate them by sending them out into the world, our hearts going with them. Don't ever forget how much energy and enthusiasm on the part of parents this will take.

REMEMBER YOUR CHILD'S FIRST STEP

I have a simple, positive message for you. Take a moment to remember how you taught your first child how to walk. Please put down the book and walk over to a mirror. Now, make that face that says, "I'm teaching you to walk." Do you remember the warmth, the affection, the encouragement packed into your reassuring smile? Now, say out loud the same words that you used in helping your ten-month-old girl take her first steps. "Come on! You can do it! I know you can! You can do it!"

Close your eyes and remember those precious times you got down on your knees, extended your arms, and encouraged your child to walk. Your face, alive with expectation and excitement, registered a winning smile. You talked baby talk and made all kinds of strange but heartwarming sounds.

When your child took two little steps and fell, what did you do? Did you lecture her? "Get up off the floor! How many times do I have to tell you that we don't walk like that in this family." "I've had it with you. You're never going to walk. You make me sick." No, of course you didn't lecture the child.

Did you punish your baby? "That's it. I'm giving you a spanking you'll never forget." "You're grounded for the next six months. You can't walk anyway. Crawl off to your room and get out of my face." Of course not. What you did was pick up the baby, hug her, kiss her, and tell her, "It's OK. You'll do better next time." You encouraged the baby to try and try again. How many times did you let the baby try to walk? We all know that you gave your child as many chances as necessary until she mastered the problem herself.

That's the nature of the encouragement that all adults possess when working with children. You've already proven that you know how to be patient, kind, gentle, understanding, and forgiving. You're a natural at this most positive parenting practice.

For some reason, parents, after successfully teaching their kids to walk, resort to a plethora of negative and ineffective parent practices. I ask parents at my workshops, "Why did you give up encouraging after it worked so well?"

There are a usual variety of answers to my question:

- "They started talking back to me."
- "The terrible twos."
- "My child developed a really bad attitude."
- "They got older and started showing disrespect."
- "They're no longer cute and cuddly."
- "They became cute and unruly."

The change in your behavior has nothing to do with the actions of your children. As adults, we're in charge of our own behavior. If we lose patience and resort to ineffective parenting practices, we should examine ourselves first rather than blaming our children.

Why do parents give up so easily? The lessons that come after walking are much harder. Children start to talk back and walk away from their parents. Some parents fall for the illusion that children can simply be made to behave. Thus, encouragement is thrown out the back door and coercion and manipulation move in and take up permanent residency.

The main reason I believe so much in encouragement is because I have experienced so many positive results. Parents really can't invest too much time practicing the fine art of encouraging. A middle school student from Manhattan wrote, "My cousin, born two weeks earlier than I, marched into a family gathering when she was four and announced that she could read. She performed for the entire gang. I knew she'd memorized the story; she wasn't really reading. But no one else realized or cared. They showered her with praise. I was very motivated to learn to read."

Encouragement is a powerful way of teaching children the important lessons of life. When it comes to life, by the way, all the lessons are important. Think of your work with children as teaching moments, opportunities for your children to develop through your kind, patient direction. Learning isn't a torture test, but a joyous experience. A woman who had raised two sons told me, "It's a hard, hard job to be a parent, but the joys and rewards are so precious. You have to concentrate on it every day, do what is right every time possible, and still feel good about what you have done even when you have doubts."

BRING ON THE CHEERING SQUAD

Being there for your children, being on their side, and standing up for them are all part of your encouraging role. As a parent, you're your child's number one cheerleader. Lead the cheers and watch encouragement work its magic.

I want to share a poem that motivates me to encourage all the children I meet for as long as I can:

> *Once upon a time I read a great big book.*
> *I mean, I read a BIG, FAT, GIANT book.*
> *And people came from all around the world*
> *Just to take a look.*
> *That's right, they came from all around*
> *The whole wide world just to take a look.*
> *And I stood up in front of the whole wide crowd,*
> *And they all yelled my name out, so I bowed,*
> *And I walked up on a mile-high stage*
> *And I opened the book and read every single page.*
> *The people clapped so long*
> *Their hands got sore.*
> *So I had to get another great big book*
> *And read some more.*
> —FROM "ONCE UPON A TIME" BY LINDAMICHELLEBARON

SIGNPOSTS FOR THE PARENTING JOURNEY

The road of encouragement beckons all parents to join the journey.
Here, then, are some signposts to look for on the path:

1. You can feel good and positive about your parenting ability. Remind yourself: "I'm a good parent."
2. You can provide your children with a consistent role model that avoids fussing, bickering, and arguing.
3. You can establish reasonable, sensible boundaries that your children will understand and respect.
4. You can have a system of routines that are easy to remember, easy to implement, and easy to follow.
5. You can teach your children basic life skills that will prepare them for success as adults.
6. You can develop intimacy and trust in your relationships with your children.
7. You can be in charge without being mean, rude, or abusive.
8. You must know what you're doing, believe in what you're doing, and love what you're doing.
9. Your children need to know they're care for, listened, to, and important.
10. Your children need all kinds of encouragement every day. Nonverbal encouragement comes in the form of smiles, hugs, and kisses. Verbal encouragement comes in the form of motivation and praise.
11. Help your children learn to get along with others from the beginning. The encouraging parent will model good interpersonal relationship skills and good conflict resolution skills.
12. Give your children an open door to your soul so they can

safely express their feelings. That's the essence of hospitality.

13. You are there to listen, support, teach, help, guide, mentor, develop, and encourage—not to judge, manipulate, and shame.

14. Families come in all kinds of shapes and varieties. There is no one "right" family.

15. Mothers have the right to choose to have both a career and children without guilt and shame being heaped on them.

CHAPTER 2

OVERCOMING OUR NEGATIVE ASSUMPTIONS
AND THEORIES ABOUT CHILDREN

EVERY PARENT HAS ASSUMPTIONS, opinions, and beliefs about children. This collection of inchoate philosophies about raising children colors and determines parental behavior. Unfortunately for children, and for parents as well, the uncritical acceptance of these traditional theories may not be good for families. To become encouraging parents, we must first have the courage to challenge some of the negative assumptions and ineffective practices of traditional parenting. Then we must be willing to jettison those unworkable, inappropriate assumptions and practices. Only then will we be able to make the move to the powerful encouraging practices that will help our children and ourselves.

There are plenty of pitchpersons for parental quick fixes, magical answers, and simple recipes. The truth, however, is that quick turns out to be temporary; magic turns into dust; and simple recipes don't work. Our problem is that we set ourselves up to spend most of our parenting time dealing with discipline. The positive, encouraging, teaching, nurturing aspects of parenting are buried in the dungeons of our minds or they're ignored. We end up forsaking our natural parenting gifts for what works for the moment, for what our parents did to us and for what makes children sit down, shut up, and stop bothering us. That's why some parents end up being mean, loud, and obnoxious. That's why parents scream at and threaten their children. Somewhere we get the wrong message that "children must do exactly what they're told or else." I have heard parents say, "It's my way or the highway." "Eat your peas or I'll shove them down your throat." "Sit down, shut up, and behave yourself." "If you ever do that again, I'll rip your arm off." "I'm going to hit you so hard your friends will feel it." No wonder there is so much conflict in our homes.

Many parents, without investing in a critical investigation of the basic nature of parenting, buy into inappropriate, ineffective, demeaning parenting techniques that have been employed in various ways for centuries. As a result, they spend an inordinate amount of time controlling children and making them mind. According to Ghandi, "The means are the ends in the incipient stage." We become more and more of what we're doing every day. If our means are control and coercion, that becomes the end product. Children can and do learn to live within these harsh parameters and even learn to obey, but the long-term effects are questionable. Before we know what hit us, we tend to allow discipline to sublimate every other positive aspect of parenting. Making children mind becomes the end goal of our parenting experience. Every waking moment is spent micromanaging our children. They're told what to do and what to think and where to sit and how to dress. Discipline becomes something done to children. We set ourselves up for frustration and constant family infighting when we concentrate on being controllers instead of encouragers.

Positive, encouraging parents don't attempt to control their children and make them mind. As Barbara Coloroso points out in *Kids Are Worth It,* "Often the result of control is either that kids become submissive, obedient, and compliant or that they go to the opposite extreme and rebel against any and all authority." Dignity and respect are lost in this method of parenting. But we have a hard time letting go of what has always been used to get children to "straighten up and fly right." As one mom told her children, "I'm going to put the quietus on you" (a quaint Southern slang expression for getting kids to shut up and be quiet). I overheard a mom having a telephone conversation with one of her children. Mom said, "I swear if you touch my computer again, I will kill you in your sleep." Any time we resort to manipulative, threatening techniques to enforce compliance, any time we control children and make them mind, we're using a set of old, demeaning, and potentially destructive parenting techniques. Making children mind is simply not the same as teaching children how to live well and get along with other people.

A number of negative assumptions about children have guided our understanding of discipline. Whenever we hit stormy weather in our families, we insist that children are all incorrigible. "Look at how kids act," the parenting consultants say. As Alfie Kohn says in *Beyond Discipline,* "What we need is strong discipline so kids know we won't put up with their foolishness. What we need is…" more of the same old discipline. "Thus, the more we discipline, the more need there is to do so." These negative assumptions become the beliefs that form our basic approach to parenting.

If you go to your local bookstore and pick a book on parenting from the shelf and review its contents, you'll be treated to a variety of ways to make children mind or make them act "appropriately."

- The "problem" with discipline is almost always rooted in children.
- Blame is universally ascribed to the nature of children.
- Parents tend to take the disciplinary status quo (tradition

perpetuated over generations by parenting experts) for granted and therefore continue to perpetuate it.

I want to put an end to the blame cycle. Children misbehave. Parents blame children for all disruptions. Parents react to misbehavior in harsh, punishing ways. Children rebel against these tactics. Parents react to misbehavior in harsh, punishing ways. Children rebel against these tactics. Parents increase the punishment. Families operate from the assumption that living together is normally a daily battle. Arguments, fights, conflicts, disagreements, and shouting matches lead to disrespect, anger, resentment, and a host of other negative feelings that now hang over the home like black clouds. The smoke barely clears from one battle and you can already hear the rumbling that signals the beginning of another fight.

The result: emotionally exhausted parents and confused children. I don't believe that parents enjoy living this way. The life of a family doesn't have to be a war. I'm convinced that there are better ways for parents and children to live together in an environment or climate of peace. Home doesn't have to be a place of unrest, stress, tension, and discouragement.

Children are not a problem to be fixed. Before we can make positive changes in the home climate, however, we need to make a critical evaluation of the negative, often unconscious assumptions and theories that underlie the majority of discipline techniques that battling families use every day. Notice if you've made any of these assumptions and how they've colored your experience with your children.

ASSUMPTION #1: CHILDREN ARE BORN BAD. IT'S OUR JOB TO TEACH THEM TO BE GOOD.

Underlying most discipline approaches is a theological assumption that children are born in sin. There are serious theological/religious issues at stake here that raise the emotional level of the debate about the nature of children. Some preachers will cite examples of the sinful, self-centered misbehavior of nine-month-old babies. Even non-religious parents may not believe their children are bad so much as uncivilized. The responsibility of the parent is therefore to get the bad nature of children under control.

The assumption of the bad nature of children arises out of a much deeper and more ancient archetypal metaphor: Life is a battle. This dominant metaphor informs much of the fundamentalist religious culture of our day. Mark Johnson, in *Metaphors We Live By,* suggests that we structure our daily reality by the metaphors we choose. Even more so, he says, we live according to a whole network of common, everyday metaphors whose power over us we rarely question. For example, "Time is money" and "Argument is war" are powerful American cultural metaphors. As we race through the day and fight battles to be number one, we uncritically accept that this is the only true and right way to live. But we're wrong. Not all cultures treat time as money or arguments as wars.

Parents across the country tell me that their home is like a war zone. They report graphic details of daily battles with their children. Without realizing what has happened these parents have uncritically accepted a metaphorical construction of reality: Raising children is war. Our job is to turn battlegrounds into places of peace by vanquishing the enemy. Thus there follow fights and feuds and campaigns of attrition and punishment. People get wounded and hurt in war. There is unimaginable pain. And yet we continue to structure our families in this way. Tight control, tough discipline, coercion, and stress along with a loss of dignity combine to turn our living room into battlegrounds.

In Rebecca Wells's novel *Little Altars Everywhere,* she writes: "It was war on all fronts. I just wish my own home hadn't been one of them. But don't get me started on that. There weren't any deferments from the battles in my house."

Should our homes be battlegrounds? How would the family environment change if we structured reality as "family life is a banquet" or "family life is a dance"? Aren't there more positive ways to structure life in families? Do we really need more "weapons" or better tactics? Do you want to be more destructive or more creative? A parent at one of my seminars responded to my insistence on creativity with a complaint, "We don't know how to dream up these cute, creative ways to discipline." She underestimated her ability. And she probably lacked the patience to try new approaches.

Once a parent buys into the opinion that children are born bad, certain discipline techniques follow. The parent asks, "How can I make my children behave?" The focus becomes one of "right" behavior. As one parent said, "I'm going to beat goodness into you if it kills you." Actually, few parents ever verbalize the assumption of childhood badness in such an obvious way. But I contend that the reason many parents keep a tight rein on their children and run their families like some kind of boot camp for criminals is their assumption that children are basically bad. If something goes wrong, the parents assume the kids did it on purpose, with malicious intent.

This dark view of human nature, this heavy burden of guilt and sin placed on the shoulders of infants, has been preached from Saint Paul to the present day. Small wonder that discipline techniques are tough and harsh when the parent begins with such a pessimistic view of the nature of children.

Haim Ginott, education professor and author, forcefully reminds parents to remind themselves: "It's my personal approach that creates the climate. It's my daily mood that makes the weather. …I possess a tremendous power to make a child's life miserable or joyous. I can be a tool of torture or an instrument of inspiration. I can humiliate or humor, hurt or heal. In all situations, it's my response that decides whether a crisis will be escalated or de-escalated and a child humanized or dehumanized."

When we choose to accept the assumption of children's natural badness, we tend to punish children and make their lives miserable. We become tools of torture. We humiliate and hurt and dehumanize our children and ourselves.

If we start with the negative assumption that children are born naughty, selfish, or aggressive, we'll look for bad intentions in our children's actions. I'm not suggesting that there is no evil in our world. I'm saying that the root and cause of evil doesn't lie in the hearts of infants. I'm saying that children are as capable of altruism, generosity, empathy, and goodness as they are of being evil, selfish, mean, and spiteful.

Children are not born in sin or inherited badness; children are simply born. They can learn to rely on reason rather than brute strength, to exhibit compassion rather than aggression. They often act in negative, hurtful ways because of the way they've been treated by adults and because they mimic adult behavior.

Children are as likely to be born with altruism in their genes as original sin. But the assumption you choose will color your parenting in very different shades. Parents who believe in the basic potential goodness of children are going to have a completely different reality than those who start out insisting that children are bad by nature, who will be on guard for every indication of their children's bad behavior.

ASSUMPTION #2: THE ONLY WAY TO CONTROL CHILDREN IS TO GIVE THEM EXACT INSTRUCTIONS OF WHAT TO DO AND WHAT WILL HAPPEN IF THEY MISBEHAVE.

Let me ask you a basic question: What is parenting for? If you assume that your job is to police every action of your children, you're buying into the assumption of control. A parent's job under this scenario is to make children mind. The three foundational principles of this approach to parenting are control, coercion, and compliance.

Let's take a closer look at the twin goals of control and coercion. First of all, this is an exhausting approach. Do you really have time to micromanage your children's every waking moment? You will need eyes in the back of your head and you will have a lot of headaches. If you're single, working, or a step-parent, you really don't have the energy for such an approach. One mom said to me at a recent parenting seminar, "I'm always worn out. My children get on my nerves and before I know what's happening, I start shouting ultimatums and threats." This mom knows that control isn't effective, but she's too tired to think of any positive alternatives.

One of the primary reasons that religious authorities and other parenting consultants keep putting working moms on guilt trips is that their controlling approach to parenting requires the constant presence of at least one parent. This leftover from a patriarchal, male-dominated society works well for men. Women and children are not treated with dignity under this system. They're still treated as property.

Once we start using control as our basic technique, we have to maintain control over just about everything, closely directing our children and providing them with activities that are highly structured. The purpose of this approach, of course, is to maximize obedience to parental authority. Children aren't asked to learn how to solve problems, provide for themselves, or think for themselves. Their task is to learn what constitutes nonconformity and avoid such behavior—to comply is to succeed. A compliant child is a "good" child.

This approach to parenting is popular in numerous parenting books. For example, the parenting manual *Magic 1-2-3* has the subtitle: "Training Your Children to Do What *You* Want." The emphasis in these books is on maintaining control. The language is borrowed from animal obedience school. The needs, desires, thoughts, and abilities of the children are virtually ignored. Children are not taught so much as controlled.

Many parents no doubt use this approach. They tell their children exactly what to do. They issue ultimatums and punishments. Their prescription is dictate, control, and threaten. Parenting becomes a monarchical dictatorship. The purpose of such parenting is to get children to do whatever they're told without question.

Parents often buy into these manipulative parenting programs because they're simple and easy to use. As one parent said, "Just tell me what to do. One, two, three. Spell it out and I will do it." No thinking involved. No problem-solving. No learning how to get along. No communication skills required.

Furthermore, I believe some parents engage in these questionable control techniques out of a desperate need for something that gets instant results. We have instant oatmeal, instant grits, instant gratification, instant everything. Why not instant compliance to parental demands? In our busy, attention-deficit dash through life, we often take shortcuts with our children rather than developing the patience to slowly teach them. We resort to tactics that deep down we find distasteful, demeaning, and debilitating. Parents often say, "We feel terrible spanking, yelling, threatening, but we have to do something."

If we want our children to take responsibility for their own actions and choices, to possess resiliency, and to solve their own problems without whining, blaming, or complaining, we must avoid control, coercion, and compliance.

Take a close look at the control, coercion, and compliance model. It involves a mindless model operating inside a human brain. There's an old navy joke that says a sailor's survival on a ship depends on the following aphorism: "If it moves, salute it; if it doesn't, paint it." The essence of human intelligence is creative flexibility, our skill in grasping new and complex contexts—in short, our ability to choose rather than to act by the dictates of rigid, preset rules. Human beings don't behave as machines with simple yes-no switches. That's a mechanistic, reductionistic approach to parenting.

Why should we take for granted that the child is always wrong when he fails to comply? What if our method is flawed? Are we punitive and controlling? Do we give children real choices? Is the ultimate goal mindless obedience? What do children learn from control, coercion, and compliance? One parent sneered, "I turned out fine. What's your problem?" Perhaps that person succeeded "in spite of" not "because of."

Ask your children how they perceive the constant use of control techniques. Talk to them about your behaviors, practices, attitudes, and assumptions. Are you uncomfortable with the constant stress that comes from badgering children to behave? Do you feel exhausted from the time demands of micromanaging your children? Ask yourself: Why? Where do these practices originate? Why am I acting this way? Are there better ways to deal with children? Why is there so much anger, hurt, and stress in our home? Why does our house sound and feel like a war zone?

The most obvious way to get a child to do as you say is to make him or her do it. The most traditional, most entrenched negative parenting technique is outright, in-your-face coercion. "Because I said so, that's why." Without regard to feelings, dignity, or future outcomes, parents often resort to coercion. In other words, the child is forced to act in certain ways.

Barbara Coloroso, in *Kids Are Worth It,* insists that parents want to influence and empower their children, but often fall into the trap of controlling them and making them mind.

> Do you want to influence and empower your children or control them and make them mind? Most of us will probably say that we want to influence and empower. But often our techniques belie that answer and very forcefully demonstrate that we're out to control our children and make them mind. We might not use brute force, but we do tell our child to go stand in the corner when she has hit her brother. Obediently she goes and stands in the corner, or defiantly she refuses to stand in the corner, forcing us to resort to other punitive measures. Either way she hasn't learned to deal responsibly with her anger, and we still won't trust her alone with her younger brother.

ASSUMPTION #3: CHILDREN WON'T BEHAVE UNLESS PARENTS PUNISH THEM OR REWARD THEM.

Punishment

Punishment is the action we take when we make a moral judgment that our kids have done something wrong. Punishment is about controlling kids, keeping them in line. It makes our kids angry. It teaches them that large people can beat up on smaller people.

I shudder when I see a parent slapping a five-year-old child while yelling, "You bad boy, don't you ever hit your brother." Or a parent who screams, "I'm going to keep spanking you until you stop crying." Why then do we punish children? I have asked thousands of parents that very question and I have received four basic answers:

1. "We don't want our children to believe they got away with something."
2. "My children have to know I'm in charge or they'll run all over me."
3. "Punishing beats doing nothing."
4. "Somehow I feel the need to win, to show the kids I'm the boss and they'll do whatever I tell them to do."

In the earliest stage of human moral development, the motivating factor in a person being good and obeying the law was fear of punishment. In the Hebrew culture of the early Old Testament period, the law of Deuteronomy prescribed punishment for rebellious children:

If someone has a stubborn and rebellious son who won't obey his father and mother, who doesn't heed them when they discipline him, then his father and his mother shall take hold of him and bring him out to the elders of his town at the gate of that place. They shall say to the elders of his town, "This son of ours is stubborn and rebellious. He won't obey us. He's a glutton and a drunkard." Then all the men of the town shall stone him to death. So you shall purge the evil from your midst; and all Israel will hear, and be afraid.

DEUTERONOMY 21:18–21

In early American history, the Puritan preacher Jonathan Edwards dangled his congregation over the open flames of hell. He told them they were suspended over hell by the thin string of a spider's web. This fear of eternal punishment kept people in line.

While we no longer stone our children to death for disobedience or give much credibility to Puritan preaching, we still use the principle of punishment. There is still the element of primitive judgment and justice in the practice of punishing children. After all, punishing children lets them know exactly who's in charge. It works for the moment, is quick and easy to impose on children, and makes parents feel powerful.

We can move beyond the elementary stage of moral/social development to a more benevolent approach to raising children. Here is an analogy to help demonstrate how this kind of development has taken place in a related area. There have been four responses to the human need for justice:

1. Unlimited retribution: If you kill my horse, I will kill your horse, your wife, and your children.

2. Conditional retribution: "An eye for an eye, a tooth for a tooth."
3. Conditional love: I love my own family, my own people.
4. Unconditional love: I forgive and love all people.

Parental punishment is more closely related to level 2—conditional retribution. "You hit your sister, so I'm spanking you." Please consider that there are more highly developed ways to respond to children. Punishment makes a child suffer in order to teach some type of lesson.

There are at least five problems with punishment:

- Punishment fails to treat children with dignity.
- Punishment fails to solve problems.
- Punishment doesn't change behavior.
- Punishment warps relationships.
- Punishment can create new problems or make old problems worse.

Punishing children instead of teaching them and disciplining them tends to multiply problems. Punishment has to be repeated over and over again. The results are only temporary. Children learn no sense of accountability. They do, however, learn to manipulate punishment. As a child, I was known to calculate my punishment for some form of misbehavior. I would do the bad deed and take my punishment. I had the feeling that I had "paid" for that particular misdeed and could now safely move on to more creative, more disruptive behavior.

The writer Harry Crews, in his autobiography, says that parents in Bacon County beat their children and they "used crying to determine when they should stop. It wasn't how loud the crying was, but a whole complexity of factors: how genuinely contrite did it sound, how hopeless, how agonized and full of grief, how well did the child understand that he was worthless and only by the grace of God and the slash of the whip, both administered for reasons of love, could he expect to get near people again..."

Many parents protest the assertion that punishment isn't effective. "So you're suggesting that when my son calls me an s.o.b., I'm supposed to ignore it and not slap his face?" No! I'm not saying that disrespect should be ignored. There are alternatives to punishment beyond doing nothing. Parents have multiple options.

If my son used that kind of language, I would make sure he understood that he cannot show that kind of disrespect for me and that profanity is unacceptable language. I would say, "That kind of language will not be tolerated in our family." Real, serious, and valuable consequences should be given to children for inappropriate language. For example, I would discipline my son in ways that I could monitor. For example, I might take the car keys and not allow him to go out for the weekend. (In chapter 9, I will demonstrate a variety of approaches to discipline that can be helpful with disrespect as well as other inappropriate behavior.)

Too often we stereotype parental responses into two tightly constricted little black boxes: punishment or permissiveness. That repertoire is too limited. Punishment and permissiveness are both formulas for disaster. But parents are afraid that failure to punish will be perceived as a sign of weakness. Thus a parent locks in punishment as the only way to convince children that it's not acceptable to act in such ways.

Punishment, then, is neither necessary nor helpful. As you teach children to become altruistic, responsible members of society, punishment only gets in the way of those goals. It also exacts an awful price. It hurts children; it damages dignity and respect. Once you punish a child, you have an uphill climb to convince that child all over again that you really do love him.

Rewards and Bribes

Rewards and bribes come in a more attractive package, but at heart they're simply kinder forms of coercion and control. Stickers, stars, candy bars, toys, and sundry rewards are given out when the parent gets the desired behavior from the child. As in punishment, rewards and bribes are adult-imposed and centered on what the parents want or demand. Children learn to get rewards by doing exactly what their parents want done.

Never rely on rewards to produce good behavior. I don't pay my children to make straight A's in school. I don't give them money for completing their chores or helping with family projects. Instead I use high expectations and real encouragement. *I want my children to do good because good is good to do.*

The whole reward system conjures up a picture of trained dolphins jumping through hoops and getting a juicy fish as a reward. Growing a thinking and caring child isn't about learning to jump through hoops to receive temporary rewards. And yet parents fall for the lure of rewards all the time.

- "If you eat all your vegetables, I'll give you a package of M&M's."
- "If you make straight A's, I'll give you fifty dollars."
- "If you stop whining, I'll take you to the mall and buy you a new outfit."
- "If you finish your homework by five P.M., I'll let you go over to Jim's house for an hour or so."
- "If you make your bed every morning for a week, I'll let you stay out late Saturday night."

While rewards and bribes are less intimidating than punishment, the goal is still control and manipulation. The child behaves in order to get paid, not out of a sense of "I want to do this for myself. This will be good for me." A lifetime of receiving rewards and bribes may leave grown children with low motivation, a poor sense of serving the common good, and a poor sense of responsibility.

The questions that rewards and bribes finally raise are:

- What do I get out of this? (What's in it for me?)
- Does it count for anything? (Do I get proper credit for doing this?)
- Did you see me? (My actions don't count if someone isn't around to applaud me.)
- Did I please you? (I'm only doing it to make you happy.)
- Did I get it right? (It only counts if I did it correctly.)

These negative assumptions and theories about children need our critical judgment. We can move away from these old ways of thinking about the nature of children and the nature of discipline. Remember: *Children are children; they're not adults.* They're not yet grown. There are developmental reasons for much of their behavior. Often they simply fail to understand what we're asking them to do; they aren't being willfully disobedient.

Dignity and respect are the twin pillars that help us subdue the storms of negative assumptions about children's nature.

1. You'll get better, longer lasting results by working *with* your children rather than doing things *to* them.
2. Control, coercion, and compliance don't teach children responsibility.
3. Punishment and rewards are *both* forms of control and manipulation.

CHAPTER 3

DOING WHAT DOESN'T WORK: INAPPROPRIATE AND INEFFECTIVE PARENTING TECHNIQUES

EVEN WELL-MEANING, LOVING PARENTS have moments when they cross the line into behavior that confuses, hurts, and denigrates their children. The stress of making a living, the personal difficulties of navigating the complex currents of daily life as an adult, and the awful exhaustion that accompanies raising children all combine to produce inappropriate and ineffective parenting. Our problem is that we resort to these techniques without thinking or evaluating them. Often, when a word of explanation and patience would do, we explode with screams and demands. It's no surprise that some of our families are in disarray.

To become an encouraging parent, we need to recognize and systematically eliminate the inappropriate and ineffective parenting techniques that we currently use. For some parents, this will require deep soul searching because old habits are hard to change. At times, the whole community seems to buy into a whole host of techniques that are harmful to children. For example, in the movie *October Sky,* a bright, visionary young boy wants to build rockets and go into space instead of working in the coal mines of West Virginia. His father, the school principal, and most of the adults in the town discourage Homer's dreams because they're themselves so discouraged, so entrenched in "things as they are." These adults see no future, no hope beyond the coal mine.

Take a look at the following checklist of ineffective, inappropriate parenting techniques. Some of these techniques you may want to argue in favor of, but I hope not. Others you never use; still others are probably your constant companions. Read the checklist out loud. For a reality check, go over the list with your children, and let them tell you which ones you're using.

☐ Sarcasm and put-downs
☐ Screaming and yelling
☐ Threats and ultimatums
☐ Lecturing
☐ Conditional love
☐ Fear and intimidation
☐ Encouraging competition

The purpose of checking your parenting techniques isn't to create guilt. It's to give you an opportunity to discover what's wrong, what's not working, and what can hurt your children. Here's the chance to take a deep breath, start over, and use more appropriate methods. If you worry about the way you're handling conflict with your teenagers, maybe you've been losing control of your temper. If you're firing off tons of advice for your five-year-old in the middle of the mall, maybe you're overreacting to the situation. The point is that you can change. Remember, if you keep doing what you have always done, you will always get what you have always gotten. I know that you're frustrated and want to create a calmer home environment. You want to relate to your children with dignity. It's worth the work to change ineffective techniques.

SARCASM AND PUT-DOWNS

Sarcasm has become the rage in our culture. We've elevated this nasty practice to the high art form of humor. Watch any situation comedy on television and note the constant barrage of sarcasm and put-downs. Watch *Frazier* or *Friends.* These shows would have no script if all the sarcastic or insulting lines were cut. This isn't an attack on comedy. Personally I love *Frazier.* It's my favorite show on television. But what's funny on television isn't funny in families. Television is fantasy. It's not real life. When parents use sarcasm or insults on their children, they're not getting laughs; they're creating pain.

Recently, Matt Groening, creator of *The Simpsons,* responded to criticisms that Bart Simpson is a bad role model for children: "I now have a seven-year-old boy and a nine-year-old boy, so all I can say is, I apologize. Now I know what you guys were talking about."

The power of language to create reality should not be underestimated. The way we talk to our children and the words we choose are crucial to their sense of well-being. There is no more important prescriptive for parents than, "Watch your tongue." If I could make and enforce one rule for parents it would be: No put-downs, ever. The writer of the New Testament Epistle of James warns, "...the tongue is a fire...a restless evil, full of deadly poison" (James 3:6, 8 RSV).

Clearly, then, we need to pay attention to the words we use and the way we say them to our children.

I have heard parents say some harsh words that berate, belittle, denigrate, and hurt children. Say the following statements out loud with the necessary dramatization. Hear the ugliness of the words and the mean spirit of the tone:

Verbal Bombs to Avoid

- You will obey me or else.
- I don't care what anyone else says, you'll do what I tell you to do.
- Shut your face.
- This is the only way.
- It's my way or the highway.
- You will sit here all night if it takes that long.
- If you act like a sissy, I'll put you in a dress.
- Eat your peas or I'll shove them down your throat.
- We don't act that way around here.
- You better straighten up and fly right.
- Sit down, shut up, and eat.
- Don't give me any of your smart lip. I'll knock it off.
- You can't wear that. Are you trying to humiliate me?
- How could you be so stupid?
- You're such a slob.
- Stop crying or I'll keep spanking you.
- You're such a wimp.
- I'm going to hit you so hard your friends will feel it.
- I'm going to knock you to kingdom come.
- Do you want me to slap your face?
- Stop crying or I'll give you something to cry about.

Our children have a tough enough time dealing with the verbal attacks, taunts, and sarcasm of their peers. The home needs to be a sarcasm- and insult-free zone. Words that hurt have no place in a parent's vocabulary. "Death and life are in the power of the tongue" (Proverbs 18:21).

With practice, you can replace words that hurt with words that help and heal:

- I love you.
- I'm sorry.
- I was wrong.
- I blew it.
- Next time it will be better.
- I didn't mean to hurt you.
- You're forgiven.
- I'm so proud of you.
- You did a good job cleaning your room yesterday.
- Thank you.

Words have awesome power. Clearly, then, we need to guard the words we use with our children in our homes. Our attitude, our approach, our tone of voice, our rate of speech, our facial expressions, our body posture, our movements, our gestures, and our volume are all communicating to children how we feel about them and relate to them. Children "see" everything, but they're not always good interpreters of what they see. They'll draw conclusions about us based on our nonverbal communication. Children pick up on these visual cues. They know, for example, if we're relaxed and even-tempered or tense and irritable just by how we hold our bodies. Modern research has confirmed what the Greek historian Herodotus said more than 2,400 years ago: "Men trust their ears less than their eyes."

Nonverbal Communication:
I See What You're Saying

How we communicate nonverbally is the subject of an area of research called kinesics. Ray Birdwhistell, one of its founders, estimates that more than 700,000 possible physical signals can be sent through bodily movement. These signals account for much of the meaning communicated by parents to their children. Communications research indicates that as much as 60 percent of our communication is nonverbal in nature, so it's helpful to have a better understanding of the advantages of positive nonverbal communication.

- Nonverbal communication provides a second, or backup, channel for getting your message across to your children. When our verbal communication confuses children, they're able to understand our intentions through our nonverbal medium.
- Nonverbal communication conveys more meaning than does verbal language. Nonverbal cues are more powerful than the verbal. Imagine a parent slapping a belt against his thigh and screaming to his son, "I love you." The nonverbal communicates a totally different message, one that trumps the verbal one.
- The parent's true personality is framed by nonverbal communication.
- Feelings and emotions are more accurately communicated by nonverbal than verbal means. Parents who glare and stare at their children communicate negative emotions that over time can build a wall between them and their children.
- Nonverbal communication does a better job of defining the nature of our relationships.
- Nonverbal communication is more honest—there is less deception, distortion, and confusion.

Research has shown that even very young children are strongly hurt by conflict—verbal and nonverbal—between their parents. Even a videotape of two adults disagreeing nonverbally can upset young children. There are ways you can lessen the harmful effects of nonverbal conflict. Here are some guidelines you should follow:

- Don't use physical aggression in front of your child. Slamming doors, kicking furniture, throwing objects, or beating your fists against the wall really scares children.
- Don't give your spouse the "silent" treatment. This includes pouting, sulking, and refusing to answer questions, staring, and glaring at one another. Your child will be more aware of the "cold, uncaring" environment than he would be of a screaming contest.
- Take a parent time-out when you're in danger of really losing it with your spouse. Say, "I need to step away to cool down. Let's talk more when I'm calm again." Or, "I am so mad at your behavior that we can't be in the same room right now. I need to calm down before we go any further with this disagreement."
- Model good conflict resolution skills. Take a deep breath, slow down, take time to cool off and say, "I'm under control. I can handle this without losing it."
- Don't assume aggressive, physically powerful stances over your small child.

To eliminate sarcasm and put-downs from your vocabulary, you might want to follow these suggestions:

- Never talk to your child when you're so angry that you can't think clearly. You can take a time-out for yourself. Take a few deep breaths and count to ten. Walk away from the volatile situation. You make bad decisions when you're mad.

- Be positive and sincere.
- Avoid making dramatic statements that you don't really mean.
- If you wouldn't want someone saying something to you, then don't say it to your child.
- Tell the truth.
- Let your child know that you're upset, disappointed, or angry without using sarcasm. You can say, "I'm so upset right now I can not talk to you." Or you can say, "I'm too mad to deal with this. We will discuss your behavior tomorrow." "I am so disappointed I don't know what to say, but give me a few minutes and I'll give it a try."
- Establish direct eye contact with your child.
- Soften your facial expression with a warm smile. It's harder to be sarcastic when we smile.
- Look at your child when you're talking to him. Direct eye contact communicates sincerity, genuineness, and caring.

SCREAMING AND YELLING

Nothing sacrifices respect in the home and poisons the environment like screaming and yelling. None of us are perfect parents and there are times when the best of parents lose it for a brief period of time. Yet if there is a common denominator among hurried, hassled parents, it's the tendency to scream and yell at their children. Before we realize what's happening, we're raising the roof in our house. All that screaming and yelling increases the stress level of parents and children. In the chaos that surely follows, children are scared and parents are frustrated.

Parents often tell me they resort to screaming because "my children just won't listen to me. They never do what I ask them to do."

As parents fall into the trap of repeating themselves again and again, what happens? Each time the parent repeats the request or the command, the volume increases and the voice gets higher. Each scream gets louder and louder. A first-grader ignored the teacher's instruction five times before calmly carrying them out on the teacher's sixth scream. The principal asked, "Why did you ignore the teacher?" The student replied, "Because my mother never means it until she screams at me at least six times."

A grandmother stands at the door and screams at her four-year-old grandson. "Stop blowing that horn." The grandson, Kevin, safely ensconced in the car, ignores Grandma, and keeps pounding on the car horn. Now Grandma gets really mad and starts screaming louder and louder. Finally her screaming leads to a threat, "Stop it or I'm going to beat you to a pulp. I mean it. Did you hear what I said? I really mean it." Notice that the screaming led to threats and the final result was a complete loss of self-control by Grandma. She took the conflict elevator to the top floor. Meanwhile, Kevin kept blowing the horn.

Screaming and yelling often are the opening blasts in family warfare. The first scream sounds like the salvo from a cannon. A child reaches for a glass, and is told, "Stop that," and then is slapped for touching the glass. A little girl is told to sit down, shut up, and be quiet. Parents, tense and upset, create the same negative, fearful emotions in their children.

A child walks in a mud puddle because it looks like fun and yet Mom screams, "Get inside, clean up, and don't ever go in that water again." I remember reading a novel in which a seven-year-old boy was convinced that you would go to heaven if you believed in Jesus and didn't play in the mud.

Children begin to feel discounted by all the parental screaming. They feel they're of little or no worth and are scared to be happy.

The whole climate of the home is poisoned by the fear of getting out of line or doing something wrong. I know a woman who keeps her house so clean you would be afraid to sit down on her sofa. When my mother made me visit in this woman's house I would sit on the edge of the sofa and hold my breath as long as possible for fear someone would scream at me if I breathed in that spic-and-span living room.

I realize that we tend to scream at our children when we're exhausted and frustrated by other more pressing problems. But keep in mind that as long as you have children at home, you're always tired. Being wiped out from hard work all week is no excuse for screaming at your children. Some parents who scream commands, obscenities, and threats like fire-breathing dragons may not know any other possible way to deal with their children. They're at the end of their rope and the quick burst of temper is such a relief. Parents who grew up being yelled at will probably have a tougher time ridding themselves of this nasty habit.

Parents use a variety of rationalizations to justify screaming and yelling:

- "I try not to scream but he won't listen to me any other way."
- "She's just asking for it, daring me to yell at her."
- "What do you want me to do? Just ignore him and let him walk all over me?"
- "My kids have to know I mean business and when I scream they know I mean business."
- "He screams at me, so I have to scream to be heard."

Are these really good reasons for sacrificing your self-respect and screaming at children? Do these rationalizations justify loss of self-control? No. We can, with practice and discipline, learn to change the nasty habit of screaming at children.

Parents can replace screaming with quiet, firm expressions of their feelings. While screaming may offer parents the illusion of power, the reality is that an out-of-control parent can't be in charge of an out-of-control child. I'm not suggesting that parents shouldn't have or show feelings. It's certainly all right to be happy, sad, frustrated, and angry. Feelings are as natural as breathing. Families will have fights. Conflict is a natural part of life. We don't, however, have to increase the resentment by screaming and yelling. As adults we're in charge of our attitudes and our actions. If we scream and yell at our children, it's not really their fault.

Screaming scares children. Their nerves stay on guard day and night. They're on the lookout for rage and explosions. They're less likely to relax and laugh and enjoy life. They tend to ignore the parent, scream back, or hide. And screaming can lead to other, more hurtful acts.

I have a series of cues that I employ if I catch myself screaming at someone else. First, I take a few deep breaths and say to myself, "I can deal with this" or "This doesn't deserve to be a verbal explosion." Sometimes I say, "I am out of control and that isn't helping anyone." Second, after calming down, I excuse myself and walk away from the situation. Third, I come back and apologize: "I'm sorry for blowing my stack. Please forgive me."

If your child screams at you, make sure you don't respond in kind. With a quiet calm voice remind your child, "Screaming is not tolerated. It's inappropriate behavior. I'm asking you once to calm down and speak to me in a quieter tone." If your child doesn't respond appropriately, you may give one more warning and then give him or her real consequences such as not playing outside for the rest of the afternoon or not watching television that evening.

One parent taught me her father's motto: "When the other person raises his voice, you lower yours." When her kids scream, she responds with a whisper, which encourages her kids to quiet down to hear her.

In chapter 9, I will deal in more detail with practical and positive ways of disciplining and teaching children the difference between appropriate and inappropriate speaking and acting.

THREATS AND ULTIMATUMS

In my travels around the country to present parenting programs, I spend part of my time visiting malls and stores to watch parents with their children. I refer to this project as parenting research. At a Wal-Mart in Greenville, Alabama, I saw a dad shopping with his six-year-old son. The youngster was into everything and Dad was about to lose his cool. Finally, Dad reached out and grabbed his son, and screamed, "If you don't stand still, I'm going to rip your arm off." The kid considered the import of these words, smiled, and grabbed a can of motor oil off the self and rolled it down the aisle. Why? Because he was calling Dad's bluff. The child recognized the threat as a meaningless piece of bluster. Dad, without realizing it, had put himself in a position of having to carry out the threat or allowing the kid to make a fool of him. Obviously, Dad was not going to rip off his son's arm even though he was capable of entertaining such a thought. Teachers often remind parents: "Say what you mean. Mean what you say. Do what you say you're going to do."

Children face enough developmental challenges while growing up without being scared into mindless obedience by their parents. The use of threats denigrates, degrades, and dehumanizes children. Sure, they may behave for a short period of time, but they do so only out of fear.

Threats are, of all things, an attempt to scare children into obedi-ence. Do you really want to use fear as a primary method of dealing with your children? The use of one threat usually produces more and more threats until the parent completely loses control. Threats also invite more conflict. Some of the most-repeated threats are:

- "Shame on you for breaking that glass. Do you want me to slap your face?"
- "You talk back to me one more time and you will be grounded for the next six months."
- "I'm going to spank you until you say you're sorry."
- "How would you like for me to put a knot on your head?"

Stop with the treats and ultimatums. Domination, manipulation, and coercion of children will compromise all your expressions of love and concern. You will damage your child's self-understanding, self-esteem, and sense of responsibility.

LECTURING

Since you have so much to teach your child, you may have a ten-dency to shake your finger in his face and give long, boring lectures that are demeaning and ineffective. If you find yourself endlessly lecturing your child, keep in mind that your kid is probably not lis-tening. His body is standing there in the room, but his mind has taken a journey to a quiet, still place where your voice can't inter-fere. Lecturing has more to do with the tone of your voice than the actual substance of what you're saying. You can tell if you're lec-turing in a negative way if your tone of voice and attitude reflect a put-down of your child. You're agitated. You're bent out of shape. You're not in a good mood. The lecture is a way of getting even with the child that you consider responsible for your bad mood. Remember, you are in charge of your own mood. Ease up on the lectures. The younger the child, the shorter your message should be. Be brief and be kind.

CONDITIONAL LOVE

In terms of lasting emotional damage, parceling out love on conditions may be the most devastating thing a parent ever does to a child. If we attach conditions to our love, we don't really love. Here we consider a subtle and significant problem: to the child a conditional reward or gift suggests a conditional love. While it's certainly okay to reward a child for some achievement with an unexpected gift, surprise, or celebration, it's not okay to use the gift as a lever, a means of obtaining the child's obedience. Then the gift, instead of proclaiming the parent's love, now suggest that the child must earn the love of his parent.

Conditional love amounts to extortion. "If you make an A in algebra, I'll buy you a new racing bike." There is no relationship between algebra and bicycles. The parents thinking they're accomplishing two goals—giving a gift and getting high achievement from their child—are actually creating resentment. The child now feels he will be loved only when he makes A's. Trust me, your child would rather not have a racing bike in order to avoid the deep resentment and pressure he would feel from trading love for performance goals.

Conditional love says:

- "I love you *if* you're good."
- "I love you *if* you keep your room clean."
- "I love you *if* you make straight A's."

- "I love you *if* you do your chores."
- "I love you *if* you sleep in your own room."
- "You'd disappoint us *if* you don't get a scholarship to play college tennis."

The child, filled with doubt about the love of his parents, won't be encouraged to do better in school, keep his room clean, do his chores, sleep in his own room, or act in any other way deemed appropriate by his parents. The contest between the parents and the child will soon escalate. Refusal for refusal, punishment for punishment, and the distance between will grow ever wider. The element of bargaining and extortion will taint the parent-child relationship.

One of the big illusions that parents have about conditional love is that money can solve all our problems. Many parents show no affection for their children except in the indirect way of spending money on them. What children need is attention, not dollars! Children need to experience the joy of "I'm loved," not the agony of "I love you if…" They don't need to win contests, knock the top off the S. A. T. examination, or prove themselves. As Erich Fromm wrote in *The Art of Loving:*

Unconditional love corresponds to one of the deepest longings, not only of the child, but of every human being; on the other hand, to be loved because of one's merit, because one deserves it, always leaves doubt; maybe I didn't please the person whom I want to love me, maybe this, or that—there is always a fear that love could disappear. Furthermore, "deserved" love easily leaves a bitter feeling that one isn't loved for oneself, that one is loved only because one pleases, that one is, in the last analysis, not loved at all but used.

FEAR AND INTIMIDATION

Some children are frightened into obedience. They learn only out of a deep sense of fear. Their mistakes are not tolerated. Their parents rule with intimidating words like "If you ever get a speeding ticket, I'll burn your license and you'll never drive my car again." "Your brother was the valedictorian of his class. What makes you think you can drag home a B in American history? Keep that up and you're grounded."

The purpose of fear and intimidation is to break a child's will. Finally, the child, overwhelmed by brute strength—physical and emotional—shuts up, keeps his feelings to himself, and tiptoes around his parents. The children in such a home appear well behaved but underneath the silence they simmer with rage, anger, frustration, and more awful fear. The glue that holds the family together is force, intimidation, power, and manipulation. For some children, this is only the beginning of a vicious cycle that will be repeated when they have children of their own.

In his memoir *A Childhood,* Harry Crews talks about the fathers in the poor neighborhood where he lived as a boy:

> Junior's own daddy, Leland Lister, almost never used any other entrance to his house except the side window after first giving himself a medium to heavy hurt with whiskey. He would immediately attack his family savagely until he'd punched them all enough to make them listen. Then he would commence to say in a broken and poorly voice that he was doing the best he could, saying that it wasn't his fault. He always ended with: "I'm just like Godamighty made me." All the men of Springfield Section went about it pretty much the same way. Daddy was neither better nor worse than the rest. He was simply one of them.

Chaney, a black worker on the plantation in Rebecca Wells's novel, *Little Altars Everywhere,* reports:

> I done heard them chilren screamin fore my eye even see what was goin on. All four of my babies lined up against the wall of that brick house and every one of them buck naked. Mix Vivi out their with a belt, whuppin them like horses. And them just standin against the red brick. Yellin and cryin and screamin, but not even trying to get away from her. Standin there, letten her beat the livin daylights out of them like there be some big invisible wall round them.

Children treated in these ways will become compliant follow-ers—easy prey for any authority figure—or they may erupt into rage that carries over into their adult lives. Fear is the opposite of love. Children don't deserve to grow up in an atmosphere dark with fear.

ENCOURAGING COMPETITION

Competition isn't an unmixed virtue. Competition is a Faustian bar-gain between parents and the drive for success. The plethora of activities that bombard our children's live would have been hard to imagine even twenty years ago. Many parents push and pressure their children. The horror stories of parents living out their own lost dreams in the athletic abilities of their children can be multiplied many times over. Childhood wasn't meant to be a stress-filled expe-rience. Children should be allowed to enjoy being young and care-free. Training can be pushed to the extreme. College football and basketball recruiters talk young people into premature agreements in obvious disregard for the rules of the NCAA. The response of the recruiters: We have to stay up with the competition. There is an inherent pressure to cheat when competition is lord of the playground. Not long ago a middle school basketball player made a verbal commitment to a major university. This kid hadn't played one minute in high school and already he was under wraps. Parents get caught up in this whole pressure cooker experience.

Visit a local baseball game and watch the parents. Johnelle was at a Little League game and heard a mom shout to her son, "You better get a hit this time or you'll not get any supper." Or check out a soccer league where parents have to be told they can't say anything when they attend the games because they're so insulting to their kids. Often parents fail to consider the insurmountable odds against their children becoming the next Tiger Woods or Randy Moss or Kevin Garnett. You need a backup plan. The best place to start: Make sure your kids have an enjoyable, stress-free childhood that doesn't involve being pushed beyond the limits of their physical and emotional abilities. Of course, there is plenty of room here between the parameters of not motivating your kids at all and pushing too hard, too fast, and too early. You have to learn to use your best judgment. How can you tell if you're pushing? Check out your own inner feelings and motivations. Why do you want your child to be a star? Is it because your child has tremendous gifts and abilities? Or is it because you want your child to succeed for you? If this is your dream and not your child's dream, let it go. Give it up. Allow your child room to breathe. Our son Kirkland is a great athlete. But he never really wanted to concentrate on one sport. It was tough for me not to push him because of my own upbringing, but with Johnelle's help, I curbed my worst impulses. Today he participates in triathlons. His childhood was happy and filled with fun.

The purpose of sports for children is to have fun. The single-minded focus on winning and competing are major problems for kids today. A kid doesn't have to win every game he plays. In fact, learning how to lose with grace is a more important life lesson.

Learning how to play and do your best and move on to the next day is more important than being driven to win.

I was raised to compete and win at all costs. Losing was not tolerated. As a member of a championship Dixie Youth baseball team, I was taught to slide hard into the legs of the second baseman on the other team. He might drop the ball and I would be safe. My coach once told me to take my baseball bat to the umpire if he made one more bad call at the plate. As a summer league baseball coach, I get a lot of static from players and parents who detest my policy of playing every member of the team in every game. Don't misunderstand. I like to win. Winning is usually better than losing. But there are other lessons that kids need to learn. Sportsmanship isn't just for losers. Help your child gain an emotional balance between the joy of winning and the sorrow of losing. Competition isn't as important in life as cooperation.

Competition isn't just on the playing fields. Take a look at the messages you send your kids. Is a B no good because it isn't an A? Is everything about being better than someone else? Do you encourage your child to measure success against peers? If everything is about winning, your child will end up losing.

I believe that all parents want to avoid ineffective and inappropriate techniques that hurt their children and sacrifice respect of the entire family. Let this desire be the initial building block that moves you to create a new foundation. You have so many natural parenting gifts. Once again, construct the mental picture of yourself at your encouraging best. Remember to take that trip back in time to the precious moments when you were teaching your child to walk. Recapture the warmth, the kindness, the encouragement of those teaching moments and bring them back to the present. Now you're ready to use positive parenting approaches with your older children.

CHAPTER 4

THE EMOTIONALLY MATURE PARENT:
DEVELOPING SELF-CONTROL

IN CHAPTERS 2 AND 3, you learned about negative assumptions and theories that people have about children that impact our parenting skills. You also learned that there are a number of oft-repeated techniques that are ineffective and inappropriate. These crucial first steps will help you overcome practices that denigrate children and turn your home into a war zone. But identifying what doesn't work isn't enough. Once you're aware of negative, ineffective, and inappropriate techniques and have determined to eliminate them from your parenting practice, you're ready to take the next important step. Change is never easy, but always possible. Knowing that you want to be a different kind of parent means changing your perspective. Now, rather than concentrating on what our children do wrong, we're going to concentrate on ourselves and what we can do right.

As someone who has surveyed the dozens of discipline manuals available to get children in line and make them mind, I want to suggest a different perspective. Parenting isn't as much about doing things to children as it's about parental self-control. In other words, if you're having problems with your child's behavior, don't leap to blame your child. Look first at how you can improve your own behavior and attitudes. I offer the following theme as the heart and soul of all good parenting; *The encouraging parent possesses emotional maturity.*

THE POWER OF EMOTIONAL MATURITY

Johnelle, my wife, is the model of emotional maturity. A public school educator for thirty years with stints as an elementary principal and a middle school principal, Johnelle has an amazing spirit of calmness around children. She has the capacity to deal with the crises dumped in her lap by children without losing her cool, sacrificing her dignity, or having an emotional explosion. This awesome emotional maturity is the formula for successful parenting.

Two seventh-graders were in Johnelle's office at Glasgow Middle School. They had been sent to the principal for fighting. Both boys were still angry. As they walked into Johnelle's office, they were still yelling at each other. As they got louder, Johnelle assumed control of the situation and talked firmly *but quietly* to both students. She met their loud, angry words with calm, soft-spoken ones. She was able to calm them down enough to explain the next steps of their conversation. Each student was given an opportunity to tell his side of the story. The first boy said, "Mrs. Kennedy, it's not my fault. He made me hit him." Johnelle worked with her two young fighters for about fifteen minutes. She helped them take responsibility for their own actions and resolve their differences. With her calm spirit and sense of presence, she defused a hostile situation. That's what I mean by emotional maturity. A less mature person would have joined in the yelling and threatened the students. The encouraging parent cares and cares deeply. Therefore she has patience, understanding, empathy, and a spirit of inner peace when dealing with children.

THE IMPORTANCE OF EMPATHY

Emotional maturity begins with empathy. Empathy means understanding someone else's feelings—not necessarily agreeing with them, but acknowledging them. You may not like it when your child expresses powerful negative feelings, but you should support his right to feel what he feels.

Because children have access to so much knowledge today, parents often make the mistake of believing that such knowledge transforms their children into little adults. Always remember that your children are children. Having information isn't the same as possessing wisdom or experience. They need guidance and nurturing and help at the precise moment when they think they're least in need of parental direction.

Emotional maturity is an active force in the lives of encouraging parents. While some parents react or overreact to the emotional bombs that their children explode in the middle of family life, the emotionally mature parent won't allow the emotions of children to dictate his or her emotional response. For example, if your child is angry, you don't have to respond with an equal or greater anger. There are times when children need to express anger openly and you don't need to respond. Emotionally immature parents often get sucked into the emotional tornado whipped up by an intense, irritated child. Now there are two funnel clouds wreaking emotional havoc in the family.

You can instead express empathy in a number of ways: "I understand how you feel. I would be angry about that too." "I know you are upset." "I've felt like that before." What matters most is that you label the feeling as legitimate, accept the child's feeling, and show the child more appropriate ways to handle his feelings next time. In these simple ways, you can avoid the emotional tornado and slowly produce a calmer family climate. Feelings aren't good or bad; they just are. Your kids need to know that it's safe to feel their feelings. Teach them the right words to express those feelings: "I'm mad." "I'm frustrated." "I feel embarrassed." "I don't like this." Give your child permission to feel.

KEEPING YOUR COOL BY BEING COOL

As parents, we're responsible for our own feelings and emotions and actions. As adults, we have to learn to take ownership of our feelings. We also have to learn how to step forward and admit responsibility for how we act out our feelings. Children don't "make" us angry. Children don't "cause us" to have temper tantrums or screaming fits. The emotionally mature parent is in charge of his or her own feelings. I'm not, however, suggesting that this is always easy. I have walked outside, taken lots of deep breaths, and muttered, as a litany, "I can deal with Jennifer" plenty of times.

As a matter of course, I developed "Daddy's time-out" as an alternative to losing my cool. My children never responded very well to the concept of time-out, the enforced seclusion for a specific amount of time. They would simply leave the time-out area and create another whole discipline problem. On the other hand, time-out has always worked well for me. When I found myself getting emotionally out of control, I would say, "Daddy needs a time-out." Then I would go to our bedroom, close and lock the door, and stay in there until I was once again calm.

This has always been an important exercise for me because I'm a very emotional person. As a child, I would get upset if my parents were a few minutes late coming home from a night out. When I'm upset, I make fast and mostly poor decisions. When I'm angry, I say all the wrong things in all the wrong ways. Rather than spend my time cleaning up emotional spills caused by the storms of my emotions, I decided "Daddy's time-out" was a far better alternative. Then, over time and with practice, I needed fewer and fewer time-outs. Emotional maturity is a habit of life that's hard-earned and not automatic for most of us. *Give yourself a time-out when you need one.*

There are a number of ways to keep your cool with children. Use these four steps to help yourself regain control. Once you're in control, you can teach your kids the same steps.

1. Walk away from the noise.
2. Take the time to calm down and breathe deeply.
3. Ask yourself some important questions: Why am I so upset? What happened the last time I was this angry? What can I do now instead of losing my temper?
4. Use the power of the smile. I've learned that a smile relaxes the tension and enables me to deal with most discipline situations without losing my cool.

TAKING YOUR EMOTIONAL INVENTORY

Another good exercise for parents is the emotional inventory. I find that while walking through the dark caverns that contain my feelings, I'm able to identify the negative emotions that can threaten my ability to deal with my children. These "bad" feelings are like weapons if we turn them loose on our children. Take a few moments and jot down the old behaviors that tend to leap out when you're exhausted and your children have stepped on your last nerve. For example, you may have a hot temper. If you recognize the fact that you have a tendency to blow your top, you can make a more conscious effort to put that weapon away, and take the time to find and use a more appropriate response.

Norman Vincent Peale used to say that your greatest weakness could become your greatest strength. I have applied that confident saying to areas of my own emotional weakness with success. For example, as a young person and as a young parent, I had trouble with screaming and yelling. Before I realized what was happening, the decibel level in my home would rise high enough to shake the windows. All my yelling and screaming created an unsafe, insecure home environment. Well, I made a conscious decision to eliminate screaming and yelling from my list of parenting techniques.

How did I accomplish such a difficult goal? I made a promise that I would not use screaming in my communication with my kids. I concentrated on developing a daily exercise that would help me keep my cool and lower my voice. I didn't want my children picking up my bad habit of screaming about everything. If you scream and yell about everything, pretty soon everyone in the family will be screaming and yelling. People will be screaming even when they're not mad or upset: "I love you." "I love you too. Now shut up and go to sleep."

Here's how I managed to work on improving my ability to talk softly and still mean what I said. My wife reminded me of the irony that children tend not to believe what parents scream at them. For children, a screaming parent is a sign of an out-of-control parent who really doesn't mean what he's saying. As I have already indicated, an out-of-control parent can't help an out-of-control child.

Next I made a list of the good, loving thoughts that families express to each other. Why should you concentrate on the good thoughts? Because the good thoughts are spoken softly:

- I love you.
- You're beautiful.
- Great job on your algebra test.
- I'm sorry.

- Please forgive me.
- Thank you.
- You're welcome.
- Next time it will be better.
- I appreciate you.
- Can we start over?
- I'm so lucky to be married to a woman as smart as you.
- I'm so lucky to have a kid like you.
- Please.
- I'm so proud of you.

Now every morning, spend a few minutes repeating these quietly spoken statements over and over. After two or three rehearsals, add some of the statements that you have been screaming at your children, but say them in the softer, quieter tone of voice. It will go something like this: "I love you. You're beautiful. Please. Thank you. Next time it will be better. It's time for bed. Get your dirty underwear out of the middle of the floor. Please take out the trash. You're smarter than that." Within three weeks, you will create a no-screaming zone within your home. You will realize that you can say what you want with firmness and authority, but without yelling.

YOU CAN CHANGE

Maybe you're thinking, "Yeah, emotional maturity. Big deal. Sounds fine, but what exactly does it have to do with raising children?" It has everything to do with raising children. Everywhere I speak, I meet parents who are out of control. They laugh and make jokes about how they lose their cool and scream and threaten their children. "I know I should change, but they just drive me nuts." "What's a mom to do? They never listen to a word I say!" "Sure I yell and scream, but that's the only way to get them moving." There is a sort of mental block that causes parents to cling to the belief that they would act better if the children would just behave. It's actually just the opposite: If you act better, your children will too. The key to a child's behavior is the emotional maturity of the parent. There is no way around this principle. We can't help our children until we're in charge of ourselves.

Choosing your response to your children's behavior is the one factor totally within your control. For example, you can get angry with your child, let that anger overpower you, and strike out in verbal and physical anger. The more appropriate response would be to notice that your feeling is a warning that something needs to change. Perhaps you have pent-up rage because you have allowed your child to behave without any discipline for a number of weeks. Perhaps you have developed a bad attitude toward a particular behavior of your child. Either way, the choice of how to respond is entirely yours.

For example, if you're angry because your child keeps having temper tantrums and whining while you are driving, you can teach him a more constructive way to get your attention and ask you questions. When your child screams a request at you from the back seat of the mini-van, you can ask calmly, "How do you ask Mommy for something?" The child may ignore your first question, so repeat it again with the same assured, but firm, manner. Your question will cause your child to stop screaming and remember what you have taught him about asking for things.

At one of my parenting workshops, I met a stay-at-home dad in Memphis, Tennessee, who uses this technique with great success. While his wife completes her medical residency, he is "Mr. Mom." On the way to the airport, we stopped at school and picked up his two children. Within thirty seconds, as Dad maneuvered in rush-hour traffic, his six-year-old son started screaming for something. Dad asked him twice, "How do you ask me for something?" After the second time, the little boy whispered, "Daddy, may I have a piece of candy, please?"

END EACH DAY ON A POSITIVE NOTE

At the end of each day, make a conscious decision to throw out the negative experiences of the day. As you review the day, construct a mental image of all the positive experiences you had with your children. For example, if during the day, you had three bad moments, you will probably allow those moments to define your whole day for you. By recounting the positive moments, you will probably come up with a dozen or more and then you will realize that you had a better day than you thought. So at the end of each day, take an emotional inventory and don't carry the negative garbage. This will help you maintain a positive, encouraging outlook; you're doing better than you thought. When you kiss your child good night, share those positive moments. You'll both sleep better!

As a child, I watched movies about cowboys and wagon trains headed west. When a wagon train got into a race for safety, people would start throwing overboard all the possessions they really didn't need. That's a mental image for me of the way parents should throw out the negative emotions that threaten their peace of mind. Instead, treat yourself to a daily dosage of Emotional Vitamin C.

- I'm in Charge.
- I'm under Control.
- I'm Calm.
- I'm Caring.
- I'm Confident.
- I'm Capable.
- I won't go Crazy today.

EMOTIONAL MATURITY AND THE
ENCOURAGING PARENT

What are the characteristics that you should cultivate to be emotionally mature? If you're tired of the ineffective results that you're getting from yelling at or slapping your children, you can benefit from an attitude adjustment. You can learn to stop the barrage of criticism and insults and instructions that you throw at your children. Do you recognize any of these statements?

- Don't touch anything in this store.
- Be still and be quiet.
- Get inside before you catch a cold.
- Don't ever do that again.
- Hurry up, get inside, wash your hands, and get ready for dinner.
- Don't talk to me like that. I'll slap your face.
- Do you want me to wash your mouth out with soap?
- Stop that crying. I've told you that big boys don't cry.
- Stop it.
- Sit down and don't you move.

Can you see how these statements reflect panic and the need to over-control? These aren't the qualities you want in yourself or your children.

Lets look at the nine characteristics of emotionally mature parents.

1. Love
2. Joyfulness
3. Peace and a sense of well-being

4. Patience
5. Kindness
6. Generosity
7. Integrity
8. Gentleness
9. Self-control

In what practical, positive ways can you incorporate and practice these attributes into your home?

Love

Love means unconditional benevolence. Love is more than a feeling. It's more than affection. True love seeks the highest good of the other person. Love is a gift that enhances, encourages, builds.

Joyfulness

You want to give your child the sense that life is meant to be enjoyed, not just gotten through. A sense of joy brings a sense of aliveness and vitality.

Peace

A sense of peace sets the stage for a family's well-being as well as their best and highest good. Peace is the optimum positive environment or climate that parents want to provide for their children. Peace overcomes fear, insecurity, and other negative emotions.

Patience

Patience isn't a kind of gritting your teeth and bearing the insolence of children. Patience is the ability to stay put in tough situations and put up with difficult people. In other words, patience is an essential part of everyday parenting. Parenting is a tough situation, and children can be the most difficult of all human beings to tolerate. When you're able to maintain a calm sense of patience and purpose, you're going to get better results in helping your children with their behavior.

For example, if your child has a habit of going to her room and slamming the door because she's mad, what is your usual response? If Jennifer got mad at me and slammed the door to her room, I'd give her that one on credit. She knew our rule about not slamming doors, and sure, she wanted me to lose my temper and have a big fight with her. Instead, I calmly reminded her of our rule, had a cup of tea, and watched *Sports Center* on ESPN. Then one night Jennifer decided to challenge my patience. She stomped off to her room and slammed the door over and over again.

Now I had to do something. I considered rushing up to her room like a stampeding buffalo and giving her a piece of my mind. Old habits die hard. Instead, I went outside and gave myself a chance to collect my thoughts and maintain both patience and composure. I decided to give her the benefit of the doubt. With a steeled determination, I went to the boat shed and got my hammer and screwdriver. Slowly I walked to Jennifer's room and knocked. When I walked in, she was sitting on the bed glaring at me, waiting for a confrontation. I managed to smile. And for me, that's the key to maintaining control. I said, "Jennifer, I see you're having a problem with your door and I'm here to help you." I took the door right off the hinges and walked out of the room without a word. For three days, I kept the door and waited patiently for Jennifer's response. Her siblings asked her, "How do you like this open-door policy?" They also started wandering in and out of Jennifer's room, taking things without asking permission. Finally, on the fourth day, Jennifer came up to me with a smile. She said, "Daddy, I love you so much. May I please have my door back?" I got the hammer and screwdriver and helped her put the door back in place. No lectures from me, no protests of unfairness from her. Patience almost always pays dividends.

Kindness

Kindness speaks of a mellowness and sweetness in one's attitude. In other words, kindness is the opposite of chafing, irking, and galling. Children need to be the natural receivers of daily acts of kindness. Kindness dispensed on a daily basis can become the antidote for cynicism or a mean spirit. There are those who recommend "random acts of kindness." When it comes to children, I would recommend regular acts of kindness.

Generosity

Generosity means basic goodness. It's a kind, strong goodness. It's a warm-spirited nature. By generosity, I don't imply a vision of dollar signs dancing in the minds of children. What I do mean is a generous spirit. A generous parent has a spirit of forbearance, forgiveness, and understanding. In this sense, parents are generous with their time. They take time with children and they make time for children. To be generous means to show empathy for the feelings and needs of your children.

Integrity

Integrity means trust, fidelity, and faithfulness. A parent with integrity has a consistent behavior pattern under all circumstances and in all places. To have integrity is to be a whole person. A person with integrity is like a solid piece of linoleum—the same all over. My dad is a model of integrity. He's an honest, caring, and consistent human being.

Gentleness

Children need gentleness. To be gentle is to be considerate. In order for children to learn how to be considerate, parents have to model gentleness on a daily basis. There is an old word that captures the meaning of gentleness—meekness. To be meek means to channel raw energy, power, and ability in the service of goodness and wellness. Parents are the teachers of meekness. When we "meek" our children through teaching and discipline, we don't break their will or their spirit. We harness their energy, their gifts, and their abilities in the service of a greater good.

Self-control

Self-control may be the ultimate parenting virtue. When parents practice self-control, they're in charge of their own volatile emotions and don't allow anger to cloud their judgment. The most important discipline in the world of parents has nothing to do with making children behave. On the contrary, the most important discipline is self-discipline. Only when parents are under control are they capable of being in charge. I'm convinced that self-control leads to self-discipline.

Parents often tell me they've tried a particular method of discipline that I recommended at my workshops and get no positive results. When I ask them how many times they tried the discipline, the usual response is, "Once, because it didn't work." Discipline requires consistent, regular application and follow-through until children understand what's expected of them. Children will respond better if parents are able to be calm, cool, and in charge. Remember, an out-of-control parent can't help an out-of-control child. As I'll explain later in Chapter 7, you need to try new techniques for a minimum of two weeks of total consistency to see consistent results.

A+ PARENTING

I believe that all parents start out wanting to be the best parents in the world. I use the term A+ as a mark of excellence. A+ parenting involves:

- Affection
- Appreciation
- Acceptance
- Affirmation
- Awareness

Affection

At first glance, reminding parents about the importance of affection sounds like belaboring the obvious. What is obvious, however, to adults isn't always as clear to children. In families where parents are hard-nosed and demand conformity by threats and intimidation, kids have trouble picking up the message of love. When parents inhibit expressions of care, concern, and happiness, the message of love can get misplaced. When children are degraded, denigrated, and demeaned, the message of love vanishes. When children rarely see their parents expressing affection for each other or enjoying life, the message of love is obscured.

As a parent, you can get so busy with the multiple tasks of living and working that you take love for granted. There are three simple ways to ensure that your children get the message of "I love you":

1. Say it a lot. "I love you." "I'm so proud of you." "I care more about you than anything else in the world." Do you really suppose that we can verbally express our affection too much? "I love you" are some of the most reassuring and helping words in our language. Saying "I love you" is especially important for dads.

2. Show it. Show your affection. Kids needs lots of hugs, lots of kisses, and lots of smiles on a daily basis. The sense of connection that children feel to their parents has a lot to do with the sense of touch. Even as they get older, children still need hugs. If your teenager acts as if he doesn't want you to hug him anymore, you can still do it and say, "Thanks, I needed that hug."

3. Spend time with your children. Maybe your schedule is complicated. After all, everyone is so busy. The "busyness" of daily life takes up almost every available moment of time. Even conscientious parents find themselves falling into the habit of allotting leftover time to their children. As the lyrics of the song "Time" say, "You can't save time for a rainy day." I wish there were a way that I could magically free up some time for you to spend with your children. Since that's not a possibility, I have a few practical suggestions:

- Use your day planner (I use the Franklin Planner) to write in all your upcoming family activities before you schedule any other appointments.
- Create your own personal space for rest, recreation, and play.
- Pick one night a week and turn off all the technology: telephone, television, CD player, radio, fax, DVD, computer, VCR, etc. Then spend the entire evening in conversation with your family. Play games. Tell stories and jokes. Cook or bake together. Just hang out.
- Take one night each week or every other week and enjoy yourself away from the children.

Another helpful way of coming to grips with the tyranny of time on your life is to write a brief autobiography concerning the meaning of time in your life. You can use the following questions as guidelines:

1. How do you spend your time?
2. What is your emotional state about time? Stressed? Anxious? Serene? Calm? Exhausted? Desperate? Hurried? Frantic?
3. What kind of shape is your schedule in?
4. How much time do you spend with your spouse? Your children? Your extended family? Your friends? Yourself?
5. If you had an extra six hours every day, how would you spend it?
6. Do you worry about time?
7. How does the expression "Time is money" make you feel about or experience time?
8. Do you feel differently about time than you did as a teenager?

Read your autobiography. How much time are you spending with your kids? How much of that is joyful time?

As you assume control over your time, you will be surprised at how much better life will treat you. Your family will think you have had some kind of religious experience. For example, early in my parenting years I was not a big fan of dance recitals. With all due respect to great dance teachers, I would rather watch ESPN than go to a dance recital. They last longer than football games; there is no halftime; and no one will give you a beer. But Melissa and Jennifer, my daughters, loved to be in dance recitals. When I attended my first dance recital, I discovered why my attendance was so vital. As Melissa and Jennifer came onstage for their first number, they peered out into the audience. Their eyes locked on mine and then the magical moment came. Like Christmas trees aflame with white, hot lights, both faces lit up with smiles that would melt glaciers. I wept from shame and pride. I understood that my daughters needed my presence at their recitals.

For years, I was caught up in the predictable rut that decreed that Dad worked long hours and Mom did all the parenting. One evening, I rushed home at 7:00 P.M. for a quick dinner. As soon as I finished, I grabbed my briefcase and headed back to the office. Melissa, about three years old at the time, followed me to the door. She hugged me and looked up at me and said, "Daddy, you come back to see us, OK?" Putting my briefcase on the floor, I turned around and came back inside the house. I spent the next two hours playing dolls with Melissa. I spent the next few years making sure that my work didn't always take priority over my children's need for my presence.

Appreciation

Your child is unique and special. That means that you should appreciate him or her for that difference. After all, different isn't bad. Different is simply different. I remember thinking after our first child was born that parenting the second one would be easier. That was one of the many illusions about parenting that I have been forced to let go of. Each child is so different. As each child grows, you learn to appreciate his or her special gifts and talents.

Appreciation is best expressed with simple, direct compliments. Give specific praise for *specific* attitudes and accomplishments. "You are a thoughtful person." "I am so proud of the way you are getting along with your brother this week." Appreciation can also be communicated with a big smile. Kids need the smiles of their parents. When your child does something she didn't want to do because you told her to, acknowledge how much you appreciate the effort. "I know you hated weeding the flower beds Saturday, but I'm so proud of you." Another great way to express appreciation is to surprise your children with unplanned celebrations. Go out together for dinner and let the children pick the place. Your taste buds will survive. The appreciation will do wonders for teaching your children about appropriate behavior.

Acceptance

Acceptance gives a child warmth, security, and safety. To accept a child is to embrace his or her limitations and differences. "You're accepted" becomes the motto of parental unconditional love. Children are accepted because they're children. No other reason is required. They've valued by virtue of being. Our acceptance of our children can't be conditional. This doesn't mean that I will like my child's choice of music or hairdo. Chances are I will like neither the music nor the hairdo.

When I participate in the parenting experience, am I attempting to get something for myself or am I attempting to give something of myself? When a parent practices conditional love, he withholds acceptance until the child meets with his approval. Examples of conditional love would be statements like:

"I love you if you make good grades."
"I love you if you keep your room clean."
"If you stop crying, I will give you some cookies."
"If you're good, I will buy you a new DVD player."

Dr. Alice Miller, author and psychiatrist, calls such communication "stoning a child with kisses." The way parents attempt to get children to behave reveals a lot about how they feel about their children. How many of us have been guilty of implying a message of conditional love to our children?

There is another approach to love that offers children the acceptance they deserve. C. S. Lewis calls it "gift-love." The goal of gift-love is unconditional acceptance. The parent expresses gift-love to enhance, empower, and encourage children. Gift-love becomes the building blocks of our children's well-being and self-esteem. They know they're loved not because we're trying to manipulate them or bribe them. They're loved because they're persons of dignity and value. Unconditional love helps children know they measure up. They're loved, accepted. They're special human beings. Children understand they don't have to be perfect to be good.

Charlie Brown, in an old *Peanuts* strip, complains to Linus about his terminal case of insecurity. "It goes all the way back to the beginning," he said. "The moment I was born and stepped on the stage of history, they took one look at me and said, 'Not right for the part.'"

Often our children, for whatever reason, feel like Charlie Brown. Despite our best intentions, they feel like born losers. At least some of this sense of despair arises from the kinds of statements well-meaning parents make: "If you're ever going to amount to anything, you have to make something of yourself." The implication is that the child isn't presently worth anything. Children often lack the ability to make good interpretations of what parents intend. As John Claypool, Episcopal rector in Birmingham, said when his parents urged him to make something of himself, "I took these words as an assessment of my condition rather than as a challenge to my potential."

I'm not attempting to heap blame on parents for the kinds of inadequate conclusions their children often draw. I am, however, reminding you that children may need overstatement of our affection and acceptance in order to make sure they get the right message. If children begin with the idea that they're not worthy, they spend the rest of their lives in insecurity trying to prove their worth.

As Claypool asks, "Do you have any idea how much energy it takes always to have to succeed and come out number one? How can you relate openly and warmly to persons when you realize that at a deeper level you're competing with them and trying to outdo them?" There has to be a better way to live than the relentless need to compete.

That leaves us with a need for reflection. As a parent, do we want to be givers of conditional love or gift-love? Are we trying to get something for ourselves, or are we intent on giving something of ourselves to our children?

Affirmation

To affirm means to praise your child for a *specific* action or accomplishment. Be honest and fair in affirming your child's worth and value. Don't tell your child he's the best baseball player in the world after he strikes out three times in a Little League game. Instead, tell him that you understand that he had a bad game. Then you can volunteer to spend some extra time pitching to him at batting practice next week. That way he knows you really care and you're ready to help him improve.

It also isn't a good idea to shower a child with hyperbolic praise for every effort: "That's the best drawing!" Children know their efforts aren't always "the best," and they'll quickly learn to discount effusive, unwarranted praise. Specific praise recognizes their true achievements and encourages them to stay on track: "You did a great job making your bed." "I like how you drew that cow." "You did well on your test—all your effort paid off."

Each of your children will be different, with different gifts, talents, and abilities. Your task is to discover those unique areas and help your child know that their gifts are special and you are proud of them. Your affirmation of each child will enable you to avoid the trap of comparing your children to each other and creating unnecessary pressure. Your son may be a wonderful piano player and your daughter may be an excellent basketball player. Affirm and value both. Most of all, make sure affirmation is a daily part of your attitude and conversation.

Here are some verbal affirmations that you can share with your children:

- "I am very proud of you because you _____."
- "You did a lot of hard work today."
- "Give yourself a hand."
- "Good for you."
- "Good job on your homework."
- "Keep up the good work."

Awareness

Watch. Listen. Pay attention. Feel. Make sure you're there for your child's emotional needs. You have to listen with your ears, your eyes, your heart, and your mind. Peer pressure can be devastating. Only parents can help a child overcome the hurt caused by the rejection of peers. Be very aware at the deepest emotional levels. If you're not naturally aware, remember that awareness is a learned skill for most people.

Awareness means asking questions. If your son, for example, is noncommunicative, don't give up. Don't ask, "How was your day at school?" Ask specific, open-ended questions like, "What did you do as soon as you got off the bus?" or "What did you have for lunch?" or "How was your history class?" Keep working in positive ways to help your son know that you care and that you are interested in him.

When Vin was in the eighth grade, his peers were verbally abusing him because he didn't play football. He never mentioned the emotional pain this caused him. One night, Johnelle heard him sobbing. She went to his room and asked him what was wrong. After a few minutes of comfort and encouragement, he said, "Mama, I'm not like the other boys."

Johnelle acknowledged his pain and made sure that Vin understood that being "like" the other boys was not important. What was important was helping him develop his own gifts. The fact that he never played football became irrelevant when Vin made a 35 on his ACT test and became valedictorian of his high school class. He graduated from Yale with honors in two majors. Today he lives in Manhattan and is a Broadway actor. We are so proud of our actor-son who never played a down of football in school. With awareness and encouragement parents can overcome peer pressure. Don't ever be intimidated by your child's peers. Be aware of the pressures and help your children deal with them in appropriate ways.

THE EMOTIONAL CLIMATE AT HOME

The encouraging, emotionally mature parent establishes and maintains a positive, warm, and caring home climate on a daily basis. The encouraging parent is in charge and knows it. Being in charge means that you know what you're doing, that you have a certain way of doing things in your home, and that you embrace the full array of parenting responsibilities.

Consistency is so vital for parents. The emotional maturity of a parent has a lot to do with doing what is right in the right way over and over again. Consistency on your part helps your children know the boundaries of behavior. One of the most effective ways to be consistent is the use of repetition. When your daughter disobeys a family rule and asks "Why are you being mean to me?" you need to give the same answer every time this happens. "I'm not being mean. You *chose* to break the rule and now you can't avoid the consequence." Consistency enables you to teach children that you can be counted on to act the same way every time. You don't argue with your children. You don't yell or scream. You calmly say every time: "You *chose* to break the rule." (I'll spell out how to set rules and consequences in chapter 9.)

Some parents live in the fantasy world that being a good parent means being a good friend to children and doing fun stuff with them. A sure sign of emotional immaturity is a parent trying to "just be one of the guys." The resulting confusion creates additional discipline problems because of your inconsistent, permissive behavior.

Parenting has more to do with inviting children to experience the joy of learning than it does with coercing them and making them behave. The parent has such a tremendous influence on the lives of her children.

An emotionally mature parent...

- is in charge of his or her own feelings and actions.
- has positive attitudes about raising children.
- creates a warm, caring, positive home environment.
- knows how to be in charge of children without being crude, rude, loud, or ugly.
- has a calm and peaceful demeanor most of the time.

Note that none of these characteristics have anything to do with your children or their behavior. As a parent, you're probably excited about raising your children well. You can't, however, be successful until you achieve a level of emotional maturity. Parenting isn't telling children what to do and making them mind.

BEING IN CHARGE OF YOUR FEELINGS AND ACTIONS

The most essential ingredient of effective parenting is the ability to be in charge of your feelings and actions. Unlike professional athletes, you don't get an exhibition season or spring practice. The first-time parent must perform the full complement of responsibilities while learning those responsibilities. That's the meaning of on-the-job training! No wonder parents often feel isolated, vulnerable, confused, and scared. They're afraid to ask for help.

Nothing really prepares you for parenting. My dad used to insist that he was taught how to swim by his older brothers. "They threw me in the river and told me to swim or drown. That was the extent of my swimming lessons." Well, parenting is rather like being thrown into the river without any lessons in swimming. Nothing really prepares you for the complicated, multiple tasks of parenting. Unlike all other jobs, where rookies and new hires go through training and orientation, gradually gaining experience and knowledge, most parents enter the wide-awake world of raising children with no training and no experience in what to do or how to do it.

You come home from the hospital with a three-day-old baby. Maybe your mother or mother-in-law stays for a few days. Then, way before you're ready, everyone goes home. Your entry into parenting is sudden and shocking.

Four days after bringing our firstborn child home from the hospital, a tornado ripped through our community. The electrical power was out for four days. Can you imagine what that was like? I didn't know the first thing about babies and now I was literally in the dark. Yet as a parent I had to perform. That's life. You have to perform immediately. You're expected to be a good parent the first day and then improve every day after that. You learn as you go. You can do it, but it can be overwhelming.

That's why I think it's so important to learn good parenting habits, skills, and routines from the very beginning. If you fall into the trap of not growing emotionally, it will be harder to change later as parenting becomes harder. Parenting can be an emotionally rewarding, exciting, and happy experience.

If you want to be an encouraging parent, you must be emotionally mature. Don't imitate people who cannot control their own behavior. You're the only person in the world who can be in charge of you. It's a powerful and awesome responsibility. One way to maintain a positive attitude is to remember that you're the CEO of the helping, motivating, caring, and encouraging business. You have loftier goals than making a child sit still, be quiet, and behave for a few minutes. Anger, frustration, getting even, fear, insecurity, and jealousy are exhausting emotions.

For example, expressing out-of-control anger to an angry child is like pouring gasoline on an open flame. When you're in charge of your own behavior, you realize that your child doesn't make you angry. *Being angry is a choice you make.* Model how to handle your anger: "Mommy's angry because I don't like messes. I'm going to take a deep breath and calm down before we talk about it." When you're frustrated from a pile of work that you chose to bring home, find a positive way to explain your frustration to your children. "I'm tired. I have too much work to do. And there's no dinner. That, my children, is frustrating beyond measure. Please help me get a handle on things tonight."

Your children can be frustrating in more ways than I can count. There will be moments when you entertain notions of getting even with them. Rather than feel guilty as if you are the only parent to ever have such dark thoughts, admit to yourself that you are really angry and frustrated with your children. I have gone to the closet in my bedroom, closed the door, beat my fists against the wall, and muttered over and over, "My precious gifts from God, my precious gifts from God." There's a difference between acknowledging your feelings and acting on them in hurtful ways.

Many parents come to my workshops to complain and whine. They're seeking justification for their inappropriate behavior. At the end of the workshop or during the break, they come forward with their horror stories. There are, of course, some parents who are struggling with children whose behavior problems are far beyond the suggestions in this book, and I always encourage them to find professional help. A number of parents, however, are simply looking for someone to tell them, "It's not your fault." They can give reason after reason why their children misbehave and fail and cause trouble. Remember, if you don't' take responsibility for yourself, no one else will. Parenting begins and ends with your emotional maturity.

BUILD SELF-CONTROL INTO THE FABRIC OF YOUR BEING

Self-control is the virtue that enables parents to be in charge of their emotions and not allow anger or self-pity or disappointment to cloud their judgement. The only person you can actually control and be completely in charge of is yourself.

Let me ask a few basic questions:

1. Do you believe that "encouraging" is the best parenting technique to use every day with your children?
2. Do you take personal responsibility for developing the inner discipline that allows you to teach your children in calm, patient ways?
3. Are you in charge at your house without being "bossy," mean-spirited, moody, dictatorial, or out of control?

4. Do you guide your children to solve their own problems, allow them to make choices, and then hold them responsible for the consequences of those choices?

5. Do you sometimes struggle with self-control issues and feel like you're just losing it with your children?

At my seminars, I ask, "Who's in charge at your house? You or your children?" At one seminar, a frustrated parent shouted out to the whole audience, "I'll tell you right now, I'm in charge at my house." Her frustration and defensiveness were solid clues that she was not really in charge. Her children had simply fooled her into believing she was in charge.

The best way to model self-control is to remember that your children are children; they're not ready for all the complex challenges of real life. The more often you manage to keep your cool, the cooler you will become under fire.

The more controlling you become, the more dependent your children become. Our goal as parents is to move our children from total dependency to maximum independence. Self-control will take us to that goal.

CHAPTER 5

THE ENCOURAGING PARENT AS TEACHER:

TEACHING RESPONSIBILITY

ALL OTHER TASKS PALE in comparison to a parent's teaching responsibilities. As teacher, the parent's task is to provide the lessons that enable children to become responsible human beings. Every parent needs to ask, "What should I be teaching my child?" Teaching children must be a conscious act, because good teaching doesn't happen by accident. You have to make a conscious determination of your teaching mission, teaching goals, and lessons.

What are your hopes? What are your goals? What are your ambitions for your children? Do you have a plan? Are you making a conscious effort to produce a certain kind of character in your children? What are your dreams? I'm not talking just about your dreams for your children to be surgeons or presidents. I'm talking about your dreams of the kind of responsible person you want your children to become as adults.

My own dreams for my children included my hope that they would obtain advanced degrees from the university, successful careers in their chosen field, and mostly, a life of joy and well-being. I've tried to impart to my children a sense of the importance of dreaming. We've shared exciting stories about famous people, places, and events. I served as the family raconteur and produced stories from my imagination into the creative minds of my children. I took them places like art museums and historical monuments. I instilled in them a sense of purpose. John Jakes, in the opening book of his *Kent Family Chronicles,* created a family creed for the Kent family: "Take a stand and make a mark." Johnelle and I have done our best to give our children that sense—that they can accomplish any goal. "If you can see it, you can do it," I have often claimed.

Our goal is to encourage, empower, enlighten, invite, and influence our children as positive teachers. Parents should know what they're doing, believe in what they're doing, and love what they're doing as they teach their children. Great parents are great teachers. They love their children. They love teaching. They love what they're teaching. And great teachers are full of energy and creativity. Using everything around them from formal teaching to daily practices, great teachers revel in the opportunity to impart knowledge and teach responsibility. Children have so much to learn and there is so little time.

Children, left to their own directions and devices, will drive any grown person crazy. The lesson plan from a child's point of view looks like this:

- Don't be quiet when you can be loud.
- Don't keep your room clean when you can have junk all over the floor.
- Don't walk through the house when you can run.
- Never close the door quietly when you can slam it really hard.
- Never pass on the opportunity to call your sister nasty names.
- As soon as your parents are completely exhausted, start a fight with your brother.

- Never go to bed when asked.
- Never be happy unless chaos rules in every room of the home.
- Refuse to do chores, homework, or favors for family members.
- Argue about everything.
- Insist on always having your way and if you don't get it, throw a tantrum.
- When a sibling walks past you, hit him.

And these are only a few of the basic social areas where children have the capacity to step on your last nerve and drive your out of your mind. The list of lessons that children have to learn from you would fill a complete book. There is so much to teach, but you have the experience and the ability to be your child's best teacher.

You should give your children an open door to knowledge. Every day is another chance to say, *"Children, start your minds."* While all children have brains, they will not develop their minds without powerful input from you, their parent-teacher. Use the power of your own imagination to turn your children on to the sheer joy of learning. After all, you are there to listen, support, help, guide, mentor, develop, and encourage. Grant Hill, star player for the Detroit Pistons, says, "Ultimately athletes, entertainers, and politicians are not responsible for raising your children. Parents have to assume the responsibility." I want to add that schoolteachers and coaches are not the primary teachers of your children, either. You are their first and best teacher. Be responsible parents and raise responsible children.

When parents drop children off at school unprepared for learning, they are placing an unfair burden on educators. One mom told me, "I didn't teach my child to read. That is the job of the school."

Nothing could be further from the truth. The school is the support system for the basic, universal teaching of the parents. Parents need to work with and support the school.

Having watched and listened to parents threaten to file lawsuits against teachers, principals, and schools, I want to add one word of caution. When your child comes home with tales of woe from school, please defer action until you have the grown person's side of the story. I'm not saying that teachers are always right, but I know how important it is for parents and teachers to be allies, not foes. By and large, teachers at school are there for your children. They're not out to get them but out to win them over. They're not trying to make your child out to be the devil. They're trying to help your child learn as much as possible. Teachers are on your side. You do your child a disservice when you always take his/her side instead of working with the teacher to help your child overcome discipline problems.

Let me ask you one basic question. When your children are "grown and gone," what are the basic lessons you want them to have learned? I suggest taking a single piece of paper and writing out a list of the basic life skills you intend to pass along to your children. Every good teacher starts with a lesson plan.

BASIC LIFE SKILLS: YOUR LESSON PLAN

Every parent's lesson plan will be unique. Here are some values you may want to impart:

I am a responsible person. I like myself. I'm a good person. I'm a person of value and worth. Until children have a good sense of their own worth, they'll probably have trouble relating to and getting along with others. The self-esteem movement of the past thirty years has emphasized the importance of children feeling good about themselves. I believe that self-esteem has two components: feeling good and doing well. I believe children will feel truly good about themselves when they accomplish goals, complete tasks, and do well in school or sports or hobbies, not when they're showered with compliments for little or no effort. Feeling good and doing well are two sides of one coin. Parents can create new problems when they emphasize only feeling good. How can you tell if you're overdoing the feeling-good aspect of self-esteem? You hand out excessive praise: "You're the best baseball player in the world." "You're the best thing since white bread." Your child knows your words lack the ring of truth. Instead of feeling better, he or she feels more pressure and ultimately feels less worthy of your respect. The best way to build self-esteem is by teaching your child to set goals and reach them. I need to add one word of caution: Start out working with small, reachable goals. Your child doesn't need the pressure of unattainable goals. As his or her performance improves, you can then set higher, more challenging, and more difficult goals.

For example, you can give your five-year-old son the task of cleaning his room. The goal for him is to pick up the toys and manage to get the room in reasonable but not perfect shape. First, set the goal: "You need to clean your room." Then, define the goal: "A clean room is one where the toys go in the toy box, the books go on the shelves, and the dirty clothes go in the hamper." As he gets older, you can add other definitions to the concept of a clean room. Then add a note of encouragement: "You are a good picker-upper. Go to it!"

I am a responsible person. At every one of my parenting workshops, I ask parents one question: "What life skills do you want to make sure you've taught your children?" While the answers I receive have some minor variations, every audience repeats one refrain with amazing consistency: "I want to teach my children responsibility." "I want my kids to be responsible." "I want my children to take responsibility for their lives, their choices, and their mistakes." "I want my children to accept the consequences of bad choices and take responsibility for those consequences." "I want my children to grow up with a sense of responsibility for the common good." "Responsibility helps children be less self-centered, and that's why I want my kids to have a powerful sense of responsibility for the world around them." "Be responsible."

Teaching responsibility is a major task for the encouraging parent. In fact, encouragement is the best way to teach responsibility. As a mother bird gives her young a gentle push out of the nest so they can test their wings and fly, the encouraging parent teaches responsibility by allowing her children the privilege of doing things for themselves.

Teaching responsibility is another way of making sure that we're helping our children grow, develop, and mature. My motto is: "You can do it!" With daily encouragement, your children will be able to spread their wings and fly. They'll gain confidence in their ability to tackle new challenges and solve tough problems. Children that aren't taught responsibility appear to lack confidence. They tend to hold back and wait for their parents to do for them what they should be able to do for themselves. I suggest that children lacking in a sense of personal responsibility are likely to experience acrophobia—the fear of heights. They're afraid to set their goals too high because they don't have the confidence of doing for themselves and learning from their mistakes.

Some parents make it possible for their children to grow up with someone doing everything for them: the lawn service mows the lawn, the housecleaner scrubs the toilets, the babysitter cooks the meals and tidies the bedrooms. There is a better way. It involves powerful principles like democracy, responsibility, and independence.

Children receive a number of positive benefits from being taught a sense of responsibility. Responsible children are those who:

- Possess a positive sense of self-esteem based on accomplishments
- Feel capable as they interact with others and get along with others
- Behave ethically and act responsibly toward others
- Respect the values of others and celebrate the benefits of a multiracial society
- Possess skill in interpersonal encounters and communication, get along with others, and develop long-term interpersonal relationships
- Develop sound work habits, motivation, and values
- Are motivated to become productive citizens, serve as contributing members of their peer group, family, school, and community
- Avoid engaging in irresponsible behavior that leads to negative consequences such as substance abuse, teen pregnancy, AIDS, etc.

The best ways to teach responsibility are with chores, discipline, goals, and a sense of achievement. You can teach a sense of responsibility through daily activities: riding a bike while following the "rules of the road," picking up toys, doing homework, completing chores, carrying out assignments, practicing good manners, and getting good grades. "Parents can teach," Martin Seligman believes, "confidence, initiative, eagerness, kindness, and pride."

I want to help you teach your children to have a positive sense of

"I can do it." I want you to endow your kids with a sense of achievement and accomplishment. The road to this goal involves far more than merely telling children to feel good about themselves. There is a more important task for parents: Teaching children to *do* well. Accomplishment produces a sense of responsibility. Children who are taught the skills of accomplishment—how to study, how to work hard, how to treat other people well, how to avoid self-destructive habits, how to manage money, how to set and reach goals, how to solve problems and how to resolve conflicts—are the children who are learning responsibility. In other words, to teach responsibility, teach "how to" skills.

Teaching responsibility goes along with the major assumption of this work: You are the lifelong, foremost, and primary teachers of children.

It's essential that you teach your children to follow through on assignments or tasks. They should learn the importance of doing what they say they'll do. They may be angry about being made to follow through, but they will learn. A young girl forgot to feed the horses. Her father came home late that night and in the pouring rain he required her to feed the hungry horses.

Give your children chores, jobs, and assignments to do. Expect them to do their share. Each child needs to be trained to handle every household task. Each week or each month, parents can vary the chore assignments. In that way, each child, like a young cook at a restaurant, is learning all the stations. With experience, your children will be able to handle bigger chores and take on additional responsibility. If you are having a dinner party at your home, give each child certain tasks. Make sure the children understand that the success of the dinner party depends upon how well they carry out their responsibilities. One of your children will be responsible for making sure the yard is well manicured: the grass cut, the sidewalks and driveway edged, the flower beds cleaned of weeds, the cut grass picked up and put in the dumpster, and the equipment cleaned and put away. Another child can set the table; even toddlers can be shown how to lay out table mats or help you spread a tablecloth or count cutlery. This is a good assignment for teaching a child about formal dinner place settings. Another child can carry coats to an upstairs room or hang them in a closet.

By encouraging your kids to behave responsibly, you avoid microparenting. Instead of monitoring and responding to your child's every single behavior, you lighten the parenting load. In other words eliminate those constant "No's," "Don't do that," "Stop it," and "For the last time don't even think it." Instead, give children all the necessary facts and allow them to make choices for themselves. With practice their decisions will become better and hence they will be more responsible. In this way, you will tie responsible actions to trust. Your children will know they're trusted to act in certain ways, and they'll learn to do the right thing.

You can also teach responsibility by allowing your children to experience the real-life consequences of their personal choices. For example, a toddler's toys that don't get put away may go to "toy jail" for a day. If your sixteen-year-old daughter celebrates getting her driver's license by getting a speeding ticket, you should hold her accountable. A good plan of discipline would insist that your daughter raise the eighty-five dollars to pay the fine, and attend the local defensive driving school. When she completes these two tasks, you can return her driver's license and her driving privileges. The lesson will be a good one, especially for young people who believe driving the car is an amendment to the Constitution.

If your child has a cellular phone that costs $24.95 a month for 100 minutes and he goes over by 150 minutes, you can make him pay the difference. If the practice of going over the minutes in the contract continues, you can simply take away the cell phone. If your child opens a checking account and bounces five checks, require him or her to raise the money to cover the checks and the extra bank charges. If the behavior continues, close the checking account.

If your fourth grader leaves his homework assignment at school, allow him to receive a failing grade on the assignment. If your teenager doesn't come home before her curfew, don't let her go out next weekend. When this approach doesn't work, you can refuse to allow her to attend the school prom or the homecoming dance. If your son is a first string basketball player and makes bad grades, don't allow him to play for a limited period of time.

As you allow your children to make choices, you should be prepared for some bad choices. You can step in if a child's choice is dangerous or immoral, but in daily experience, allow your child to fail. You can then hold them accountable for their choices and actions even though there will be a cost in emotional pain for you and for them. Discipline that teaches children responsibility can be more painful than any spanking. To paraphrase a verse from the New Testament: "For the moment, all discipline seems painful rather than pleasant; later it yields the peaceful fruit of responsibility to those who have been trained by it" (Hebrews 12:11, RSV). Parents need the inner strength to allow children to experience the real-life consequences of bad choices and bad behaviors.

Giving your children an allowance is also a good way to teach responsibility. Children will learn to save money for those clothes, toys, and games they think they must have. They will also learn to be responsible with money by learning that "money doesn't grow on trees" (as my dad used to say at least twice every day to me).

Another good way to help your children is by defining in everyday terms what you mean by responsibility. For example, a responsible person:

- Shows up on time for work and appointments
- Works hard
- Does more than the minimum
- Keeps his or her word
- Treats others with respect
- Pays his or her debts on time, whether they're promises or bills
- Supports the community
- Takes care of his or her family

Following through on promised discipline is another good way to teach responsibility. Some children respond better to "tell and show" demonstrations. You tell them what you will do in terms of discipline, and then you show them that you meant business. When you let children off the hook for bad behavior, you not only send the wrong message, but you also give children excuses for the next day. Being held accountable helps produce responsible children. With consistent practice, you can refuse to accept or give credence to the propensity of your children to blame others. You can listen to the litany of "It's not my fault" without caving in to this advanced version of a toddler's whining. For example, when a sixth-grader blames a failing grade on "the worst teacher in the whole school," you can ask: "What part did you play in making this grade?"

I accept that part of the normal communication of most children is to blame and complain; it's how kids naturally express their displeasure at circumstances, discipline, and parents. I have learned to listen to these complaints and deflect them without being sarcastic. If one of my children blames someone else, I ask, "Tell me why you feel that you have no responsibility in this matter?" Or, "I understand how you feel, but this is a problem that needs your personal attention."

Children who learn responsibility are much better equipped to be successful human beings. Teaching responsibility is your top priority. In fact all the life skills that follow are directly related to the daily teaching of responsibility.

If your five-year-old daughter has temper tantrums and hits her brother, you probably can't solve that problem all at once. You can help your daughter set a goal of not hitting her brother. Work on one behavior at a time. Then you can add goals for not yelling, not having a temper tantrum, and then teach your daughter how to share her feelings.

I can solve my own problems without whining, crying, or blaming others. As I've said, a favorite ploy of children is to blame others for whatever goes wrong. "It's not my fault" sounds like a litany for children of all ages. "It's not my fault. He made me hit him." "It's not my fault. My mother didn't give me my medicine today." "It's not my fault. I'm a dysfunctional human being." "It's not my fault. It's El Niño mixing up my brain waves."

Breaking the whining habit requires your patient persistence. First, you should allow your child to whine only in a specific place. I suggest that you put a rocking chair in the corner of the living room. Acknowledge your child's feelings, but don't otherwise respond. Your child can rock and whine until he or she calms down. Tell your child, "I'll talk to you about your concern as soon as you stop whining." If your child leaves the rocking chair and is still whining, send him or her back. Whatever else happens, make sure that your child receives no reward for whining. If your son whines for cookies, he gets no cookies. Whining is an inarticulate plea by children to remain dependent on their parents. Instead of empowering whining, empower problem-solving and taking care of business. Ask, "What could you do instead of whining to get what you want?"

If your child blames others, remind him that he is responsible for his actions: "You chose to do this, no one else made you. What else could you have done?" Encourage him to brainstorm acceptable options.

I know to work hard. The tendency of parents to overprotect and spoil their children cheats children out of learning the value of hard work. There is no free ride. Children need to learn from their parents not to expect anything they've not struggled, sweated, strained, and stewed to achieve. Achievement, accomplishment, and activity are important elements in the upbringing of children.

For example, if your child has a term paper due at the end of the semester, you know he or she will have a tendency to put off the project to the last minute. You however, can help your child divide the term paper project into a number of smaller goals and deadlines. That way, your child can complete one section of the project each week.

Remember to let your child experience the consequences of not doing the required job. Don't rush to the school with the forgotten band instrument. Don't download the research from the Internet. Don't rescue your child from learning the important lessons that arise from not taking responsibility.

I try not to quit. Here is a lesson that my dad taught me which I have, in turn, passed along to my children. We have a motto that says, "A Kennedy never quits." At first I was rigid on this point—no giving up, ever—but I have modified the principle over the years. I now simply ask my children to consider the pros and cons of any decision they make about quitting. I ask them a few thought-provoking questions: Is this important to me? Is it worth the struggle, the sacrifice, and the sweat that I am enduring? Will this matter to me when I am ten years older? A hard-and-fast rule about not quitting does not always hold up under the scrutiny of every single experience of life.

When Melissa struggled as a first-year elementary teacher, she wanted to throw up her hands and quit. Instead, we talked it over and together we said out loud, "You know a Kennedy never quits." The reasons for staying were important enough for her to keep teaching. She loves children and she loves teaching. This is her profession. In Melissa's case, quitting would have been detrimental to her sense of well-being. She knew she would have regrets about quitting ten years from now. She knew that teaching mattered too much to give up on it now.

When Jeffrey wanted to quit the track team because he was tired of running, I at first said no. He was angry with me and wanted to know why he couldn't quit. "I'm eighteen years old!" he shouted. "I can do anything I want to do." "You're overlooking an important family principle," I reminded him. "I know, I know," he said. "A Kennedy never quits." We talked about the importance of hanging in there. I asked Jeffrey to consider all the factors and make his own decision. I told him that he would always cherish the memories of being on the track team. Either way, I would support him. Jeffrey completed the season. He ran the 1600 meters and I attended his track meets to offer my encouragement. It turned out that wanting to quit had been Jeffrey's overreaction to a bad practice. After he worked out his feelings, he was happy and, more important, he was having fun again. I was so proud of him for not quitting, but if he had been miserable running track, I would have let him quit. The important thing is not to let your children quit after only one try or only part of one season. "You can finish the season and then you can choose not to be on the team next year." When children learn how to make decisions about quitting or staying, they're better prepared to face the more difficult challenges of adult life. They also learn how to make their own decisions, not merely echo your wishes.

I realize that winning is not as important as having fun and par-

ticipating. Jeffrey taught me that I was wrong about winning. Now, Jeffrey doesn't have a competitive spark anywhere in his system. Unlike his hyperactive, ultracompetitive father, Jeffrey has never expressed much interest in winning. He would finish fifteenth in a race and smile and say, "Let's get some pizza." All the way to the pizza parlor, I would be fuming (in silence, of course) about the fourteen guys that beat my son across the finish line. Well, I realized that I, not Jeffrey, had the problem.

At the remaining track meets of the season, I positioned myself 200 meters from the finish line. As soon as Jeffrey came into the range of my extremely loud voice, I would shout, "Catch that kid in front of you." At one track meet, he even caught and passed two other runners. That was the way I managed to salvage my own competitive spirit. Jeffrey did what he did because he wanted to do it; my encouragement was a support, not a command. Jeffrey was out to have fun, not win.

I recently read about a soccer mom who attacked a teenage official; a football coach who ended up in the hospital after arguing with another coach; a father who sued his son's baseball coach for not winning enough games; and a father who raced out of the stands to slug a fifteen-year-old soccer player in the mouth. Have parents forgotten that when kids participate in sports that the goal is having fun? The horror stories of parents living out their own lost athletic dreams in the athletic abilities of their children can be multiplied many times over. Training can be pushed to the extreme limits of endurance. As more and more parents push their children to the edge of despair, it's no surprise that 70 percent of children give up organized sports by the age of thirteen.

To allow yourself to get trapped in the world of stars and bucks and glamour is to live in a world dubbed by sociologists as "the world of hyperreality." This fake world of television and celebrity status is loaded with dangers for children. Hyperreality exaggerates the importance of athletes in all phases of human experience. Television coverage and advertising support and perpetuate this illusory world where children can be everything, have everything, and go anywhere they want.

I cherish my memories of a fun-filled childhood. Always teach your children to have fun. My dad was the hardest-working man in the world as far as I could tell. Yet every day he came home, picked up his old catcher's mitt, and played catch with me. He taught me to enjoy fishing. He took me hunting, and although I no longer own a gun or go hunting, I remember that life was good. My dad taught me that *"life as it is given is good."*

I can think for myself. Children who are always told what to think are not capable of making important distinctions about right and wrong. They're prone to follow any demagogue with enough charisma and gift of gab to lure them along for the ride. They have trouble solving problems and standing up to others. The ability to think critically and solve problems go hand in hand. Teach your children *how* to think, not *what* to think.

Children learn to think for themselves when you allow them to make decisions for themselves. For example, you can allow your four-year-old daughter to decide what to wear to preschool. Who cares if it doesn't match? You can allow your twelfth-grade son to make his own plans for spring break. When children make good choices, you can reward them with more freedom. If they make bad choices, you can discipline them by taking away some of their choices.

I have respect for all other human beings. I treat people who are different from me with dignity and respect. As the musical *South Pacific* suggests, "You've got to be taught to hate." In a diverse world, you will want to teach your children that different isn't bad;

different is simply different. The lessons we have learned in the past forty years about civil rights and diversity have to be repeated in every generation.

In the movie *Tombstone,* a fictionalized account of the life and times of Wyatt Earp, there is a scene from Wyatt's childhood that sticks out in my mind. The Earp family is having dinner. Wyatt's dad says to his children. "There's family. That's all there is." And he goes on to tell his boys that no one else counts outside that little family circle. In a sense, Mr. Earp was right. There is family and that is all there is. But the circle has to be an ever-widening circle. There is only one family and that is the human family. Make sure your children learn that basic value in a constantly changing world.

Our children attended public schools in Louisiana with a diverse cultural mix in students. One of our kids came home from school and asked, "The kids at school are different colors. Is that bad?" I picked up a box of Crayolas and showed them to my daughter. "There are lots of different colors in this box and each one is important to the overall beauty of any picture you create." I did not try to create color-blind children; I tried to teach them that color creates a beautiful world. Each culture brings something positive to the world that makes the world a better place.

A congregation where I served as a minister for six years gave me a queen-size homemade quilt as a going-away present. Each piece of the quilt had the names of each family that made up a part of the congregation. The many-colored quilt pieces had been sewn together by a group of ladies from the church. I have shown this quilt to my children on occasion as an object lesson because my quilt of many colors is one of my treasures. It reminds me that many people "sewn together in threads of mutual respect" can make a beautiful world.

Peter said, "Truly I perceived that God shows no partiality, but in every nation any one who fears him and does what is right is acceptable to him." (Acts 10:34) Teaching children to respect others is a big parenting role. Teach your children that as members of one human family, family is more important than race, class, gender, or sexual orientation. Teach children about the nature of human sexuality in all its manifestations, including homosexuality.

Consider for a moment the torture and the pain that many middle schoolers go through as they struggle with issues of sexuality. Their journey is often one of the blind leading the blind because of the repression and the oppression related to sexuality in our culture. Imagine trying to help your teenager understand why he is so different from all the other boys. I want to suggest that the laws of love take priority over religious teachings or social biases. We must teach our children to accept people and themselves as they are. "Not until the sun excludes you do I exclude you," Whitman wrote.

Is it too much to ask that parents teach children to be decent and fair and that they treat people who are different from them with gentleness, dignity, and respect? Demonstrate to your children that you will never be a party to racial, ethnic, religious, gender, or sexual orientation jokes or slurs or practices that degrade other human beings.

Rather than teach your children the same old, tired arguments that homosexuality is a crime or a sin, teach them that homosexuality is merely different. St. Paul says, "For as many of you as were baptized into Christ have put on Christ. There is neither Jew nor Greek, there is neither slave nor free; there is neither male nor female; for you are all one in Christ Jesus." (Galatians 3:27–28, RSV)

The church has a sorry legacy of being wrong on so many of the issues that it once spoke with certain dogmatic certainties. If you want to have a shock to your senses, read sermons written and proclaimed from southern pulpits in the years 1800–1860. You will find detailed, tortured exegesis that professes that God ordained slavery and that owning slaves is morally justifiable. Scripture verses are quoted, arguments are put forth, and emotional appeals are abundant in the effort to justify slavery. The church has been wrong so often on so many issues. Yet the lessons never seems to be learned as each new generation of Christians hammer away at yet some other social issue that is deemed to be "ordained of God." With a history of being wrong, isn't it at least possible that we can have the humility to consider that dogmatic assertions about the nature of homosexuality may also be wrong?

You can teach your child that proofs offered in loud and emotional rhetoric by preachers doesn't equal any proof at all.

If you child discovers that he's gay, your support will be essential to his well-being. You can help him learn that homophobic fears aren't the same as truth. Christians of nearly every denomination insist that homosexuality is a sin; as a Christian, I have felt an obligation to investigate the teaching of the Bible about homosexuality. In reading the proof texts usually presented as factual evidence of the sinfulness of homosexuality, I discovered that biblical writers had no concept of a sexual orientation other than heterosexual. I was impressed with the absence of any teaching about homosexuality in texts that matter most to the Jewish and Christian tradition. For example, there is no mention of homosexuality in the Ten Commandments. In the Gospels, Jesus never mentions the subject.

People shouldn't have to live in shame because they were born a certain way. We should help our children and the world learn to respect people without regard to race, culture, gender, or sexual orientation. Respect, dignity, and love can always overcome fear, hatred, and judgmentalism. Why would Christians, people commanded to live in harmony with all, to love their enemies, to accept the outcast, to extend hospitality to strangers, insist on causing so much pain in the lives of people who are merely different?

BASIC BELIEFS

Teach what you believe from A to Z. Values, philosophy, politics, religion, and commonsense principles—all of these ideas have to be passed along to your children. As Dr. Seuss reminds us in *On Beyond Zebra,* children don't know as much as they think they know: "It's time my friend that you were shown that you really don't know all there is to be known." While children have access to tons of information, this doesn't translate into knowledge and wisdom.

The most important way to pass along your beliefs is through "embedded practices"—the routines of everyday life that define a family. Children catch beliefs more from example than instruction. That's why I'm convinced that the crucial issue in parenting isn't the behavior of children but the behavior of parents. For example, a parent who exercises self-control and anger management is more likely to handle children's temper tantrums successfully. The message that children receive when parents remain calm and under control is more important than parental lectures about getting along with other people.

If children don't know what you believe, you send them into the world with an empty slate that will now be filled by others. You rob them of any meaningful points of comparison when they confront new and often contradictory truth claims. I never ask my children to believe exactly as I believe, but I have worked hard to give them a basic set of beliefs as a starting point.

One of my friends suggested that I was overbearing about the importance of teaching children beliefs. He said, "I let my children make up their own minds about everything. I'm not dogmatic. I never take them to church. They can decide all that religious stuff when they get older." I countered, "That's fine with me. Your son may grown up to marry my daughter Jennifer and she will convert him to her well-defined liberal Democrat point-of-view. How does that fit with your rock-ribbed Republican convictions?" Don't be timid. Teach your children basic beliefs and trust them to make good life decisions.

CREATING POSITIVE LEARNING ENVIRONMENTS

You create an atmosphere that expects children to do well. Take care to offer sincere praise. Create a home environment where children want to do well. Your home becomes a place of security where no one makes fun of children. Your children feel comfortable and confident. They're more likely to take risks because they're being supported and encouraged by their parents. For example, instead of fighting with or lecturing your children about homework, create a positive space where learning is expected and homework is fun.

Homework has a better chance of being fun when you make it clear that you have positive expectations of your children. You create a home climate that communicates the value of homework. You make sure your children know that you are partners with their teachers in making sure they learn. From the first days of your child's life, spend pleasurable hours reading to him or her. As soon as possible, point to the pictures in the book and allow your child to tell the now-familiar stories. This is the beginning of reading for a three-year-old. Remember to dramatize your own reading of stories to create that sense of the sheer joy of learning. If you convey to your child that she is smarter than she thinks she is, she will be smarter.

Make sure that you don't treat your own daily chores as drudgery. Your children will catch those negative attitudes from you. If you get your children involved in chores at an early age and teach them to value the daily routines of life, they are more likely to do homework without complaining.

One of my favorite approaches is inviting my children into the wonderful world of learning: "Tell me about your assignment." "How can I help?" I invite my children to enjoy their homework with "corny" dramatizations: "Welcome to the thrills and chills of the fabulous world of science. Tell me why pigs can't fly! For that matter, explain to me how hummingbirds can fly backward and look like tiny helicopters."

I'm not naive enough to believe that children will always enjoy homework. But if you work hard to create a pleasing, happy, and positive climate, you are more likely to get results. And don't be distracted by complaints. Your children somehow believe that complaining is part of their original job description. Deflect complaints with positive statements: "I understand how you feel. Homework is hard, but you can do this; let me show you how to get started." "Charge! You have the homework mountain to climb!"

Avoid these negative killer statements that discourage your children: "Why do I have to tell you to do your homework every night?" "You never finish your homework!" "Do you want to grow up to be an idiot?" "You'll never amount to anything." Encourage instead: "Cool! You're figuring out multiplication!" "I'm proud of you; you figured that out all by yourself."

USING A VARIETY OF TEACHING METHODS

Educators often remind us that children learn in a variety of ways. There are three principal learning styles: visual learners, auditory learners, and kinesthetic learners. Children who are visual learners do best by seeing objects, lessons, and principles. With the overwhelming impact of television, the majority of children are visual learners. Lecturing to a visual learner won't be sufficient to teach them the basic lessons of life. Auditory learners do best by listening and repeating what they've heard. Kinesthetic learners absorb knowledge best through touch; they're the ones who take radios apart to see how they work. Observe your child to see which learning style suits him or her best. Adopt what you have to say to that style, and encourage your child's teachers to do the same.

Object lessons can be helpful. Johnelle often tells the story of her daddy giving her a candy bar. He told her to divide the candy bar and give part of it to her brother Bill. So Johnelle cut the candy bar into two pieces. The larger piece made up three-fourths of the candy and the smaller piece one-fourth. Johnelle had every intention of getting the larger piece. Then her dad, John Wallace, told Bill, "You pick the piece you want." Bill, of course, just as lacking in a sense of Solomonic fairness as Johnelle, chose the larger piece. From then on, Johnelle says, "I always measured the candy bar and made sure we both got exactly equal pieces." The really good news is that object lessons about values live in the memories of children forever.

Children will feel more positive about their abilities and self-worth when teachers provide sincere and requisite support and encouragement. I also believe that it's important for parents to teach children how to do tasks rather than doing tasks for children.

You can teach your children how to care for the flowers in the yard, how to clean and put away the tools, how to change the oil in the car, or how to load the dishwasher. If your child doesn't do something right, teach the skill again. Remember that our paradigm for being an encouraging parent is to teach every skill the same way you teach walking. Don't fall into the common parenting trap: "If you want something done right around here, you have to do it yourself." Recapture that loving, positive mindset: "You can do it! That's the way!" Let your children learn by doing. Even if it takes longer and you have to grit your teeth not to appear impatient.

PRACTICAL SUGGESTIONS FOR PARENTS

1. Develop strong bonds with your children. Intimacy doesn't happen by accident. You don't become close to children simply by being in the room with them. Intimacy is a dialogue, a two-way street. Taking intimacy for granted is thus an invitation to strained relationships. Strong bonds can be produced through encouragement and affection. One of the common complaints of grown people is the appalling lack of closeness and intimacy they experienced from their parents growing up. "We were total strangers," one woman told me. "My parents didn't have a clue who I was or what was important to me." Intimacy can be nurtured in special times spent with your children. Stories at bedtime are a good way to build intimacy. Having a picnic and playing outdoors with your children is also a good idea. Expressions of affection with your spouse and your children will help develop intimacy.

2. Identify and build on the strengths that your children demonstrate. Rather than having strict assumptions about what you want your child to do, take the time to find out what his or her strengths and desires are. One child may love football or golf. Another child may enjoy art or dance. Let them show you where their passions and strengths lie, and help them build mastery. It's best to give children the opportunity to experience a variety of challenges and then have the patience to see how they react.

3. Help children overcome the fear of failure. "You can do it." Once again, we have to possess the patience to teach and motivate our children in the same way we taught them to walk. There are children who lack confidence in their ability. The confidence and ability of their peers intimidate them. The difficulty of new challenges overwhelms other children. I was afraid of learning to swim as a child. The only reason I ever jumped into the water was my dad was already there waiting for me. And he held out his strong arms and said, "Come on, Rodney. You can do it." In no time I was swimming like a duck. Let your kids see you fail, pick yourself up, and try again. Don't try to present yourself as a flawless superparent. Help them learn to fail successfully by learning from their mistakes and moving on.

4. Help children overcome rejection of success. There are times when your children will be underachievers because their peers don't consider good grades and success cool. As odd as it seems, there are places where kids take a reverse pride in being poor students. The pyramid is turned upside down and the successful, popular students are considered those who make bad grades and cause trouble and get suspended. Parents have to find ways to negate such negative peer pressure and motivate their children to embrace success. While you can never completely eliminate peer pressure, you can make sure that your positive voice is always offered as an alternative to peer pressure. Young people in middle school, especially, desperately want to be popular. And making good grades can be a detriment to school popularity. Your children must sense that doing well in school is an essential part of their bright future. Once again, your job is to create the positive principles of learning. Remind your children that school is a place to gain knowledge and become successful. The more you support your child's education, the greater the child's chances of overcoming peer pressure and making good grades.

5. Help your children give up "perfectionism." If you are obsessive-compulsive, make every effort not to pass along this insecurity to your children. Some children, even if their parents aren't pushing them, will grow up with a deep sense of insecurity. A friend of mine told me that he spent his entire youth and young adult life trying to prove that he was a person of worth. No one ever got the message through to him that he was worthy simply because he was. He was convinced that he had to achieve something great to be considered valuable. Sam Keen says that when the idea of his own value finally dawned on him, "I felt like man riding an elephant looking for an elephant." Teach your kids that perfection is an unattainable, undesirable goal.

6. Help your child develop good homework and study skills. You can set the tone for good study skills by giving homework priority. A simple message usually does the job. "No television, no playing outside, and no video games until all homework is finished." If necessary, go ahead and check the homework to make sure it's finished. If your child repeatedly tells you "I don't have any homework," pick up the telephone and call his or her teacher. Don't worry if your child says, "What's the matter? Don't you trust me?" Don't be intimidated by this little ploy. Make the call and say to your child, "Every day you say there's no homework. That doesn't seem right. So I'm checking with your teacher."

7. Communicate your high expectations. No matter how your children perform or react, make sure that you hang on to and maintain your high expectations. Nothing is more harmful for children than parents giving in to failure and poor performance. If you find yourself shrugging and wanting to give up on your child, take a deep breath and recommit yourself to one basic principle: Never, never, never give up on a child. Articulate your expectations. For example, if your child hates school, demand that he or she keep going. One of our children hated school. He started the third grade with the observation, "I want you to know I'm doing this under protest." With his protest duly noted, we jump-started him every semester all the way through five years at the university. Today our son is a teacher.

You should have and communicate great expectations. "I'm so proud of you. I'm so proud to be your daddy. Let me remind you that, as your daddy, I expect a lot from you." For parents, there are only two kinds of expectations: positive expectations and negative expectations. An expectation is part of the definition of hope. Hope is desire plus expectation. When I say, "I hope my children will do well in school," I mean that I have the desire for them to do well and the expectation that they'll do well. Expectation gives voice and life to the desires and dreams of parents.

What are some of the positive expectations that you have for your children? Are you prone to lower your expectations? I believe that expectations have to be verbalized, demonstrated, and repeated. Children catch and comprehend the message of positive expectations when we say out loud what we expect. Announce your expectations: "Say it out loud, sister." Demonstrate and explain your expectations. Then repeat all of your expectations on a regular basis. A positive belief that all your children will be good people and succeed in life is the starting point for parental expectations. If you expect your children to succeed, you have personally put down the first building block of their future success. Your expectations become the cornerstone of your children's future success. From you they'll learn to be aware of ways to be successful. And it all begins with positive parental expectations.

Children have a better chance of being successful when their parents have high expectations. The odds are greater that what you want to happen will happen because you will be expending energy to see that this will be so.

Avoid words that hurt children and lower their expectations of success.

- You are dumb.
- You are stupid.
- You are no good.
- You will never amount to anything.
- I didn't want you in the first place.
- You never do anything right.
- You are such a slob.

As an anonymous poet put it:

Boys flying kites pull in their white-winged birds,
But this you cannot do, when you are flying words.
Thoughts unexpressed may someday fall back dead.
But God can't kill them once they are said.

Parents can reverse the negative results of low expectations with some specific actions:

- Make direct eye contact that's caring, sincere, and encouraging.
- Give children direct comments about specific behavior. For

example, you should say, "You didn't finish your home-work yesterday," rather than "You can never do anything right."

- Describe your own reactions rather than your child's behavior. "I'm disappointed in your behavior," rather than "You mess up so much I don't know what to do with you."
- Express genuine concern for the feelings and needs of your children.
- When a child misbehaves, deal with the problem immediately rather than waiting until the end of the day. For example, don't say, "You just wait until your daddy gets home." Say, "I expect politeness from you. Here are the consequences."
- Be attentive to developing genuine rapport with your children.
- Communicate your desire to build up rather than tear down your child's self-image.
- Model sensitivity and compassion for your children. "I know it's hard for you to do this, but I'm here for you."
- Take every opportunity to establish one-on-one communication with each child. "Let's talk after dinner about how to do that assignment."
- Praise your children for specific accomplishments. "I like how carefully you drew that map."

Good parenting is more invitation than coercion. Encouraging parents invite children to learn and grow and succeed every day.

8. Establish a learning environment where children believe learning is fun. Make learning as much fun as possible. Open your children's eyes to the sheer joy of learning. If you can make learning an adventure, your children will make the journey into knowledge on their own. Stop and explain everything to them. There is no lesson that is unimportant. A trip to the grocery store can be a math lesson. Encourage your child to wonder where the mail goes after pickup. Let your kids interrupt you with their questions.

9. Strengthen relations between your home and your child's school. The school is your ally, not your adversary. So often, parent/teacher interaction falls to Mom. I believe it's crucial for Dad to visit the school and talk with the teacher when a child is doing poorly in school or having behavior problems. Research indicates that Dad can have a greater impact on improving the child's behavior and performance. I'm not sure why this is true but kids tend to do better if Dad shows up at school. Perhaps younger children have a perception that Dad will be tougher to face. If your son's fourth-grade teacher calls you at home and says, "I need to tell you that your son, by himself, has me considering early retirement," make an appointment to see that teacher in her class the next day. Make sure Dad takes off from work, in the middle of the morning, and goes to his son's class. Walk into the class. Don't even look at your son. Spend about three minutes talking with the teacher. Leave the classroom without ever looking at your son. The nonverbal message— I'm here to communicate with the teacher, not the child—will be powerful.

When you get home from work that evening, your son will want to know why you came to his school. This will be your opportunity for a heart-to-heart talk. You can reinforce the powerful nonverbal message communicated by your personal visit.

10. Read to your children every day, and let them read to you. Make this special time sacred. No phone calls or interruptions. Don't let it become a struggle. This is a relaxing time for togetherness, not a rigid time for word drills.

11. Don't be afraid to teach family and moral values, so that

your children can become role models for tomorrow. Tell your kids what you believe in. "In this house, we _____."

BE A LEADER

Encouraging parents want to grow and become true leaders of their children. They inspire their children, motivate their children, and help their children succeed. They're self-motivated, self-disciplined people who contribute to the quality of life, first their own and then that of their family. Encouraging parents pass on family culture, customs, and traditions to their children. Encouraging parents are their children's best and brightest hope, the ones who dream of a brighter future for them. A character in one of Louis L'Amour's novels says, "Give them tomorrow."

Leaders begin with respect for their own worth. Our children need models of success. Commitment, dedication, and hard work make a person a leader. Accomplishment begins with parents who are leaders. Success of any kind requires you to take responsibility. Striving, working, praying, maintaining the highest expectations, looking after the smallest details, and going the extra mile—these are the values children need from the leadership of their parents. You can do it. It's up to you. The ultimate satisfaction lies within you. You're the teacher.

> One hundred years from now it won't matter.
> What kind of car I drove,
> What kind of house I lived in, what my stock portfolio
>   contained, what my retirement fund made in interest, or
>   what my position at the corporation was.
>
> Nor will it much matter how much I had in the bank account,
> Or what my clothes looked like,

Or what my golf handicap was,
Or how many awards I won.

But the world will be a better place because
I was important in the life of a child.
(IN HARRY WONG, *THE FIRST DAYS OF SCHOOL*, ADAPTED,
MY EMPHASIS)

CHAPTER 6

COMMUNICATING WITH CHILDREN

WORDS HAVE POWER. Something decisive happens when we speak words into existence. It's my contention that when we address our children in authentic ways, something of significance takes place. Of course, any form of human communication can be trivialized and misused. Like Eliza Doolittle in the musical comedy *My Fair Lady,* parents and children can say, "Words! Words! Words! I'm so sick of words." The complaint sounds familiar bells. In a world cluttered with words from television, radio, CD players, and cellular telephones, our own words can get lost. Whatever the cause, the words of parents are suspect. One parent said to me, "Talk to my children? I've talked until I'm blue in the face. Talking is a waste of oxygen. Words are futile and irrelevant to my children. I swear what I say goes right over their heads." I can't deny that a lot of parental talk has been of little or no value. Abuse of words, however, is never a reason to abandon a necessary and important process.

I believe that when parents faithfully engage their children in positive communication, it has the potential to make a real difference in their lives. "You're so good in math. You would make a great engineer." "I know you can do it." Communication is a skill worth doing well because of its enormous potential. After all, children understand the world from the beginning through sounds and words. Young children are social individuals. Much of the sense they make of the world comes from their communications with other people. Communicating helps children clarify their thinking and sharpen their understanding.

I used to marvel at the extended period of dependency that we humans grant to our offspring. All other mammals give their young a short period of time to grow up and get out on their own. We allow our children to hang around and hang around. Then one day it dawned on me that children is primarily for language acquisition. Within a span of about thirty months, children learn language. Babies hear words and then begin to speak words. Between the ages of two and three, children typically put together a working vocabulary of more than a thousand words. Through words, children learn to name the world.

Have you noticed how when people see a baby, the first thing they do is start talking to him or her? Total strangers walk up to babies in airports, supermarkets, and malls and start babbling away. Indeed, our first teaching consists primarily of talking.

Johnelle provided running commentary for our children on a daily basis. Whatever she was doing, she explained it to the children. If she was making New Orleans seafood gumbo, she told six-month-old babies how it was done. Start your talking early and keep up a steady stream of description, explanation, definition, and commentary. Tell your children everything about the world around you.

Your children will talk at an earlier age and develop a larger vocabulary if you talk to them. I came home from work one day and four-year-old Jennifer greeted me with, "Dad, you look rather *placid* today." Even with understandable parental pride, I think *placid* is a pretty good word for a four-year-old.

By the way, your talking shouldn't come to an end when your children learn to talk. We have a tendency to teach children to walk and to talk and then clap our hands and say, "Thank God that's out of the way!" We then begin to tell children to be quiet, sit still, leave us alone, and stop running. From somewhere deep in the parental subconscious there comes an old adage, "Children should be seen and not heard." That's simply not true. Children must be heard in order to learn. Your kids will do better in school if you work regularly on improving their verbal skills.

Educators tell us that reading to children may be the single most important contribution we as parents can make to our children's educational success. I agree, and want to add how important it is to allow your children to read out loud to you. A child will develop a larger vocabulary and become a better public communicator if he or she practices reading out loud at home.

How important is talking, reading, and telling stories? A U.S. Department of Education survey shows that mothers spend less than thirty minutes a day talking with their children. Other reports indicate that fathers spend an average of fifteen minutes a day. I don't believe that this lack of quality communication time is the result of neglect but the product of busy parents taking their children's verbal skill development for granted.

Parents are exhausted when they get home from a full day of work. By the time they finish dinner, watch the news, check the stock market, browse the Web, put in a couple of extra hours of office work, talk on the phone, return messages, and watch their favorite shows, there is precious little time left for talking and reading to children. Many families sit in semi-darkened rooms, stare at the television for four hours a night, and chalk all that up to quality time spent with the family. Sitting in the dark staring at the television creates strangers. The silence impedes the development of family intimacy and closeness.

Sure, you're tired. Every parent in America is tired. That's the normal state of parenting. There's a television ad that suggests that when you get married and have children, life slows down. The minister officiating at the couple's wedding leans into the camera, smiles, and says, "Yeah, right!" Being tired is no excuse. You're going to be tired until the last child leaves home. There's no excuse for not talking to your children.

Through talk, children learn about the world. They learn what it means to live in a family that honors empathy, compassion, honesty, and forgiveness. They learn how to think for themselves and solve problems. They learn about caterpillars, butterflies, stock options, computers, sunshine, rain, hurricanes, and politics. Talking is teaching; so open your mouth and start babbling away. You have so much knowledge, and the quicker you share it with your children the faster they'll learn.

WORDS THAT ENCOURAGE

My mother used to tell me, "Watch your mouth, young man. I'm going to wash it out with soap if you keep talking like that." In her own way, she was trying to teach me that what we say makes a difference. Well, parents need to watch their words around children. We have tremendous power to put down or to build up. From our words children will decide if we're for them or against them. With words we build a whole world of reality for our children.

Words are power and parents must learn to treat them with respect. Words can be used as weapons. Words can coerce. Words can hurt. Words can lie. At the same time, suspicion of language can't be allowed to sour our sense of wonder. With words we can also help and heal. We can motivate and encourage our children.

Author-philosopher Sam Keen says that the greatest gift a parent gives to his children is "the gift of delight." He traces the idea of delight to the ancient religious concept of blessing. Religion often contains blessings and curses. These verbal constructs offer us a way of understanding the power of words. For example, Jacob blessed his son Joseph with these words: "The blessings of your father are mighty beyond the blessings of the eternal mountains, the bounties of the everlasting hills; may they be on the head of Joseph, and on the brow of him who was separate from his brothers." The opposite of blessing is cursing. Here is a sample curse from ancient times; "Those who surround me lift up their heads, let the mischief of their lips overwhelm them! Let burning coals fall upon them! Let them be cast into pits, no more to rise!" With our words we bless or curse our children.

From various sources, including Sam Keen, parenting consultant and author Barbara Coloroso, numerous teachers, and our own home, I have compiled a list of encouraging words. I call these statements "the daily dosage of delight."

- I believe in you.
- I trust you.
- I love you with all my heart.
- I'm so proud of you.
- You make my heart sing.
- You're listened to.
- You're appreciated.
- You're welcome in my heart.
- You're on the right track.
- You're doing a great job.
- You did a lot of hard work today.
- You can do it.
- Now you have figured out how to do it.
- Good for you.

- Fantastic.
- Keep up the good work.
- Terrific.
- I have never seen anyone do it better.
- Wow!
- I knew you could do it.
- You're very good at that.
- Nothing can stop you now.
- You're a fast learner.
- Thanks for being such a sport.
- Congratulations.
- We had a wonderful day.
- That's precious.
- I'm counting on you.
- Thanks for finishing your chores.
- You mean the world to me.
- Thanks for trying.

CREATE YOUR OWN
"DAILY DOSAGE OF DELIGHT"

You can create your own "daily dosage of delight" with your own special words of praise, commendation, and encouragement. Always keep in mind that children are deeply influenced by our moods, assumptions, attitudes, and language. The ultimate desire is to build up rather than tear down.

What is your goal as a parent? Why did you have children in the first place? Exactly what are you trying to do when you communicate with your children? Perhaps you're intent on getting your children to do certain things. Your goal in this case is to make children behave. I would like, however, to suggest a more beneficial message to communicate to children. I suggest that our goal as parents is to build a relationship of love and trust between ourselves and our children. Relationships of the deepest kind are the true business of parents—to build and maintain a spirit of honest, caring, openness, trust, and togetherness.

Every day events and situations occur in the lives of the family that threaten to disrupt the spirit of trust. Mistrust, anger, greed, jealousy, and a whole host of negative emotions can take root and disintegrate and alienate families. As a parent, it's important for us to side with trust rather than suspicion. We need to believe the best rather than the worst about our offspring. Whenever we side with the negative feelings it's no surprise that all kinds of chaos breaks loose.

I want to share with my children the joy of aliveness. Life as it's given is good. I want my children to believe this same philosophy. I want them to taste something of the ecstasy and joy of life. Therefore I communicate to my children a sense of creativity. I want to give something of myself to them so that they too can know the joy and goodness of life. I'm convinced that the miracle of language is the best avenue to teaching our children the joy of life.

Tell Your Stories

The best use we can make of words is to use them in the construction of our stories. Storytelling should be a large part of your time with your children. Our children hear our stories and gradually grasp their identity. All through their young lives, children need to hear our stories until they can begin to tell their own stories. Family stories define us and ground us and draw us closer to one another—for example, how Granddad came to America from Ireland; how Mommy met Daddy; what Granddad did in Australia during World War II; where Daddy was born; how Daddy played baseball. Then we add other stories: "Right there in the front yard of Grand-daddy's house there was a huge hickory tree. That tree was my tree of dreams. I hit rocks with an old broom handle and imagined I was playing in Yankee Stadium in the World Series." Through the years our stories connect us to all our family members: past, present, and future. Our stories tell us who we are and where we live in the world. Story confers upon us the honor of identity.

I believe that telling stories is especially important for fathers. It's been my experience that mothers have a more natural intimacy with their children, perhaps from carrying the baby for nine months and giving birth. Many dads have to work a little harder to create that sense of closeness and oneness. Stories are a good beginning. With stories you will be able to give your children intimacy and independence.

So, at the very least, help your children know who they are with the stories they tell. Children rooted in a knowable past can better grow the wings that will enable them to fly. Stories help children experience intimacy (roots and connectedness) and independence (wings and autonomy).

COMMUNICATION BUILDS INDEPENDENCE AND INTIMACY

What is the nature of independence and intimacy? Independence means the ability to stand on your own two feet, think of yourself, and solve your own problems without whining, complaining, and blaming others. It's the ability to make your own choices and accept responsibility for your own life. Intimacy refers to close relation-ships with your children. Intimacy suggests generosity and creativ-ity in developing a powerful personal relationship. Sharing is a vital part of intimacy.

In order to establish independence and intimacy within the family, we must have a positive self-concept. Our own inner security will largely affect our willingness to allow others to maintain independence and to gain intimacy. If we don't feel self-love, we will have difficulty loving others.

In *Communication in the Family,* Virginia Satir explains:

> A person with low self-esteem has a great sense of anxiety and uncertainty about himself. His self-esteem is based to an extreme extent on what he thinks others think of him. His dependence on others for his self-esteem cripples his autonomy and individuality....His low self-esteem comes from his growing-up experiences which never led him to feel that it's good to be a person of one sex in relation to a person of the other....A person with low self-esteem has high hopes about what to expect from others, but he also has great fears; he's only too ready to expect disappointment and to distrust people.

Our children need us to care about them passionately and unconditionally if they are to thrive. For parents, this means overstating and dramatizing the depth of our love and affection. As I've said, children are rather poor interpreters of what they see and hear. They often draw the wrong conclusions about their worth.

Encouraging rather than critical messages may lead to lower levels of aggressiveness, fewer antisocial behaviors, greater independency, and higher self-esteem. Communication thus matters and it matters a lot. Here are five ways to improve your communication.

1. Take time to communicate. Busy parents often take communication for granted. To overcome this tendency, stop and answer every question your children ask. Take the time to explain everything in great detail. Always keep in mind the power of repeating yourself. You may feel bored answering the same question for the tenth time, but your child is learning through your repetition.

2. Give family members a full hearing. Your children will need your help in sorting through all the feelings they have. No matter how trivial your child's complaint or how confused his or her feeling, make sure you give a complete and fair hearing. Otherwise your children will believe their feelings don't count. Their feelings shouldn't be ignored, denigrated, or demeaned. Their questions should be given full and undivided attention. You need a button that reads, "GOT QUESTIONS? ASK ME."

3. Send clear messages. Talk to children in ways they can comprehend. Make sure your verbal message agrees with your nonverbal message. For example, if you say "No!" to your child with an apologetic smile on your face, the child will not believe you actually mean *no*.

4. Accept other family members as they see themselves. With a sense of awareness, you can see how your children perceive themselves and think about themselves. Rather than trying to change your children into your own image, allow them to be themselves. Encourage the development of the uniqueness that belongs to each of your children.

5. Avoid communication that is critical, evaluative, humiliating, judgmental, or sarcastic. Humiliation is a powerfully destructive influence on another person's self-concept. A child who's subjected to frequent humiliations from his parents will come to feel that he's worthless, and thus doesn't deserve any better treatment. Another destructive consequence is that the humiliated person, adult or child, will feel anger and resentment toward the humiliator and, instead of trying to correct his behavior, may concentrate his energies on how to "get even" with the humiliator. A third destructive consequence is that when you use rude and disrespectful language, you're at he same time telling the other person that you're a rude and discourteous person. This teaches children to be rude and discourteous.

THE COMPLEX COMMUNICATION
SKILLS PARENTS NEED

Think for a moment of all the communication skills required to raise children. The list will transcend any Introduction to Communication course you took in college. To help you grasp the complex nature of communication, review the following list of communication skills and see how good you are at each one.

1. **Negotiation: the art of arriving at a solution that both parties find fair.** For example, one of my children received a speeding ticket on the same day she got her driver's license. We worked out a solution that we both considered fair. I asked my daughter to raise the money to pay the fine and to attend safe driver's school. On my part, I agreed that upon completion of her end of the bargain, I would return her driver's license and restore her driving privileges.

2. **Persuasion: the method of convincing someone of your point of view without coercion or manipulation.** As a parent you are a persuader. I have used my persuasive powers to convince my children that smoking is detrimental to their health. While my children probably all experimented with smoking, none of them are smokers. Persuasion requires that you use your credibility, your powers of reason, and your emotional power. Your children will be alert to how well your words match your actions.

3. **Mediation: the ability to work out a disagreement.** If you are engaged in a dispute with two of your children over a fight that you didn't see happen, you can hold a family court in which each side

gets to state its case without interruption. As a family you can reach a consensus.

4. Reasoning: the ability to apply logic to any given situation. Instead of saying to your children, "Because I said so," give logical, understandable, and reasonable answers for your actions whenever possible.

5. Listening: the ability to hear with concentration, compassion, and empathy. Put down that newspaper. Turn off the television. Put away your work. Pay attention to what your children tell you.

6. Conflict resolution: the ability to find a solution to problems that two parties are having. Since your children will need good conflict resolution skills for the rest of their lives, you should teach them how to resolve conflicts as early as possible. Begin by helping your children understand that conflict is natural. Then you can teach them how to accept each other's point of view and then they can learn how to cooperate and compromise.

7. Counseling: the ability to offer information and advice without bias. There will be times when you will serve as your child's counselor. Remember to listen. Don't rush in with your opinion. Avoid proscriptions and find ways to help your child come up with a plan for solving his or her own problem. At times your best counseling work will be listening and understanding. Children are not always asking for answers or solutions. Sometimes they just need the reassurance that you really are there for them.

8. Evaluation: the ability to weigh information and options objectively. When one of your children comes home with a story about his involvement in a school fight, you will need to carefully consider all the facts as well as your son's feelings before reaching a decision about your response.

9. Interpersonal relationships: the ability to communicate with

other members of your family. Remember that relationships don't happen magically but with effort and presence. Get to know each of your children in personal ways. The process of building a relationship is one of discovery. I learned, for example, that Jeffrey responds better to me sitting and saying nothing rather than bombarding him with a series of questions. Melissa likes to talk through her feelings with a lot of emotion. Jennifer prefers to cut right to the heart of the matter. Vin is quiet and reflective. Kirkland is compassionate and very conscious of the feelings of others.

10. Small group relationships: the ability to communicate with several people. A family is a particular kind of small group. Your task as a parent is to help your small group work together to achieve your agreed-on goals. Remember that a small group functions better when every member of the group has status and voice. Help your children feel confident about their place in the family and make sure they have a legitimate voice. You will not always do what your children request, but you will always want to allow them to have a voice.

11. Information exchange: the ability to convey important information. One of your big communication tasks is passing along information. If your daughter says, "That's not fair," you give her the universal fact: "Life is not always fair." Information can be as simple as explaining how you expect your children to act at dinner and as complicated as how you expect them to get along with each other.

12. Rapport: the ability to connect with other people in caring ways. You establish rapport with your children through conversations, stories, games, and working together.

13. Self-disclosure: the act of showing and telling other people who you really are. Tell your children about yourself. Communicate your feelings, your dreams, your fears, and your hopes. Open all the windows of your soul and allow your children to know you as the real person you are.

14. Imaginary interactions: a communication strategy that helps people anticipate encounters with others in advance. In an imaginary interaction you can rehearse an upcoming moment of discipline and make a more rational decision about any necessary actions on your part.

While all of the above listed communication skills are important for parents I want to expand on our understanding of three of the more essential skills.

LISTENING

Listening is a primary skill in communication. You have to listen with ears, eyes, mind, and heart. I believe it's important for parents to learn how to trust their inner feelings or spirit. Perhaps I should call it PI—parental intuition. Listening is a positive parenting practice. The encouraging parent is a listening parent. There is no way that we can stay in touch with our children without utilizing our listening skills. Watch and observe. What do your children like? What do they choose to wear? Who are their friends? Are their grades good? Are they reaching their potential? What are they watching on television? What are their major interests? Listen and look. Feel your child's inner spirit. Watch for signs of laziness or inertia. Watch for indications of irresponsibility. Attitude is everything. Listen for the attitude that your child has toward life. Is it a positive, optimistic attitude? Does your child catch the purpose of life? Does your child understand that life as it's given is good? As a parent, one of the most positive parenting practices is sharing the ecstasy of life. Help your child catch the spirit of life's basic joy.

The best listeners have the best eyes. Good listening skills enable parents to recognize, understand, and remedy misunderstandings with children. Why? Because when parents truly listen they're not judging, criticizing, evaluating, or demeaning their children. They're taking the time and making the effort to understand what their children are saying.

In a world of noise and interference as well as a plethora of conflicting claims of truth, listening is no small task. Communication theorists remind us that "interference" or "noise" is the stuff that gets in the way of effective communication. As parents, we have to learn how to tune out the distractions, put down the newspaper, turn off the television, and forget about work in order to concentrate on listening to our children.

There are three basic kinds of listening: ignoring, automatic pilot listening, and compassionate listening. We often ignore our children without realizing it. After all, we're so busy, so distracted, so stressed out. There is so much to do and so little time. Our children talk to us and we keep right on doing whatever we were doing. "Put down that newspaper and listen to me" is almost a universal cry from children and wives.

When children are ignored, they're hurt. The hurt may not be at a conscious level, but over time they begin to feel demeaned and left out. To ignore children then is to deny intimacy.

Automatic pilot listening is nothing more than pretense. We appear to be listening but our minds are on that project deadline at work, the upcoming marathon race, bills that are due, or the rise and fall of the stock market. Our children are too smart to be fooled by pretend listening. It hurts just as much as ignoring them. Research indicates that men are more likely to engage in automatic pilot listening.

I know a guy who pretends to listen to his wife each night by saying "yes" or "uh-huh" every fifteen seconds. He says that he doesn't have a clue what she's saying. He also doesn't have a clue that his pretense is building a wall between him and his spouse. Ignoring and pretending are twin destroyers of intimacy.

Compassionate listening means that we put aside all distractions, all judgments, all assumptions, and listen to our children with all our heart and soul. We understand where they're coming from and how they feel. Real listening is hard work and takes all our senses operating at maximum capacity. A lot of energy is expended in listening. Perhaps that's why so many of us are such poor listeners. No wonder Alice Walker writes, "Every woman secretly wants to marry a giant ear."

This is a marvelous image for parents. We serve as giant ears for the hurts and concerns and needs of our children. We make a space for them in our hearts so that they know they're loved, understood, and listened to.

Listening allows us to provide helpful feedback. How often do conversations turn into arguments because we're not paying attention to the legitimate feedback of our children? We argue with our children about feelings as if we know exactly how they feel. In unconscious ways, we act as if we always know exactly how they feel. In unconscious ways, we act as if we always know exactly what our children are thinking, how they're feeling, and how they should act. As one child put it, "My mother says she just wants me to be happy—doing what she wants me to do."

If we're not paying attention, our thoughts will become self-absorbed. We will lack the emotional energy to put ourselves in our children's place. I'm not saying that it's easy for parents to tune in to what their children are feeling or thinking. Sometimes the effort is like trying to find an AM radio station late at night that plays your favorite jazz. Most of the time you hear a lot of static. I don't believe that the verbal technique of paraphrasing or mirroring what our children say to us about their feelings ("What I hear you saying is...") is sufficient, although it's a good start. What I have in mind is more like a complete change of perspective or point of view. Being in touch with the feelings of other people is far more than a mere verbal technique. Words like empathy, compassion, concern, understanding, and acceptance come to mind.

As parents, we tend to deny a lot. We're like lawyers at trial, constantly shouting "I object!" "Don't you dare say that!" "Don't ever let me hear you say that again!" "How dare you talk that way about your grandmother!" Parents can get stuck on automatic denial. Our children will sense that we're not listening when we keep denying their feelings.

Listening involves far more than hearing. We actually have four sets of ears. We hear with our biological ears. We listen with our eyes. With our mind we're able to hear and interpret the meaning of messages. Our hearts allow us to interpret the emotional messages we receive.

A Lesson in Listening

Some years ago I learned a valuable lesson in listening. Johnelle came home from school and announced, "I have had the worst, most horrible day at school in my entire career." With my limited listening skills, I was on the verge of saying something less than empathic like, "You think *you* had a bad day! Let me tell you about *my* day." I was saved, however, by Rita Boyd. Rita and Ed, our two best friends, had stopped by for a visit. Before I could say anything, Rita walked over and hugged Johnelle. What she said was a powerful lesson for me. "I understand how you feel. Start at the beginning and tell me everything."

I'm slow but I'm not stupid. I went to the bedroom and wrote on a slip of paper, "Start at the beginning and tell me everything."

One day I figured that saying would be useful. Well, about six months later, Johnelle came home and said, "I'm so exhausted. Nothing went right at school today." Thanks to a good memory, I walked over, hugged my wife and said, "I understand how you feel. Have a seat in the den. Let me get you something to drink and then you start at the beginning and tell me everything."

Johnelle smiled, kissed me gently, and said, "That's so precious, but I know where you got that." Well, it didn't matter, because she gave me three points anyway. The lesson in the value of real listening was not lost on me. I vowed to learn to be a great listener for my wife and for my children.

"Start at the beginning and tell me everything." Put this phrase into your own mental notebook. The next time your child bursts in to tell you about the latest tragedy, stop yourself from offering advice, solutions, scolding, or punishment. Stop and say instead, "Start at the beginning and tell me everything." Then listen, really listen.

Good listening can have a profound effect on conflict between parents and children. When parents stay calm and see conflict as an opportunity to help their children grow, they will be more likely to listen. If your teenager explodes because you have asked him to clean his room, you can take the time to listen to his side of the story. Sure, you'll be treated to a bombardment of excuses and irrational explanations. You will, however, gain credibility because your son will learn that he can safely express his feelings and that he has a right to his opinions. In addition, your son will watch you model good conflict resolution skills and slowly begin to emulate you. There is a lot to be said for using your ears and your mind before opening your mouth.

SELF-DISCLOSURE

I have come to believe that genuineness is a critical quality for parents; anything unnatural and artificial blocks the parent's credibility with the child. Being genuine and natural means relaxing and being yourself. The best way to accomplish naturalness is through self-disclosing communication. I suggest "self-disclosure" and "genuineness" are synonymous.

You have to decide whether to allow your children to know you as you really are. Otherwise, parenting becomes a game of hide and seek. To some extent, this is a false dilemma, because parents reveal themselves in every word, every attitude, and every action with their children. Their nonverbal communication speaks volumes to their children. After all, children miss very little of what goes on around them. But since they're very poor interpreters of what they see, they need your verbal explanations.

What is self-disclosure? I define self-disclosure as the opening of the soul to others. We peel away the layers of pretense and show ourselves as we really are. We take off our masks and live as genuine persons. You practice self-disclosure by revealing information about yourself to your children. The most effective way of revealing such information is through the telling of stories. Funny stories, sad stories. Mistakes, triumphs, scary times, good times. The more stories you tell your children about yourself, the better they'll know you. There will be more intimacy and more connection between parent and child.

If your family isn't an open, honest place, it's not really a family at all. If you aren't a model of genuineness, then your children have no one to guide and teach and encourage them. If we can't know and be known in our family, how can we ever practice honest, openness, and love for one another? Self-disclosure is vital to the emotional health of the family. Self-understanding, personal growth, and interpersonal relationships are all dependent upon self-disclosure. Yet, according to Gerard Egan in *Interpersonal Living,* "Intimate self-disclosure doesn't seem to be the norm in most American families." And as Frederick Buechner says in *Telling Secrets,* "Maybe nothing is more important than that we keep track, you and I, of these stories of who we are and where we have come from and the people we have met along the way, because it's precisely through these stories in all their particularity that we make ourselves known to others most powerfully and personally."

Guidelines for appropriate self-disclosure:

1. Practice self-disclosure in all areas of family life.
2. Use self-disclosure to accomplish the ends of your teaching.
3. Tell your children stories of your own success and failure in life. Avoid bragging about your vices and mistakes.

The Johari Window

Parents can evaluate the scope of their self-disclosure by using a tool from communication theory called the Johari Window.

	You know	You don't know
Your children know	OPEN	BLIND
Your children don't know	HIDDEN	UNKNOWN

The window represents what each person in a family knows and doesn't know about one another. The panes of the window contain the information about the self that's available for sharing or disclosing.

The Open area: The first pane contains knowledge about yourself that everyone knows. This is shared information that's common knowledge in the family. "You know how Dad is. He loses his temper." "You know how Dad is. He's so affectionate." The information in the open area may be feelings that you have disclosed to your children or it may be behaviors that your children have observed about you.

The Blind area: The second pane consists of aspects of your life that your children know about you, but that you don't know about yourself. Everyone has blind areas. Here is the home for your prejudices, biases, assumptions, and attitudes. You also have mannerisms and other patterns of behavior that you're unaware of, but every member of your family knows about them. For example, my children would say to me, "You don't have to yell at us." I would reply, "I'm not yelling. I'm talking to you in a normal voice." I was totally unaware of how loud my voice really was.

The Hidden area: All those things you know about yourself but never share with your family or friends make up the hidden area. Sometimes we're afraid to reveal secrets. Usually there are a few skeletons in the closet. That hidden area is what you know about yourself that no one else knows.

The Unknown area: The last pane represents information about you that you don't know and your family doesn't know. This is your potential growth area. The unknown area is a reminder that life is a journey into the not-yet-known.

Self-disclosure consists of enlarging the open area while shrinking the blind, hidden, and unknown areas. As you disclose more about your true self to your children, you will become closer to one another. You will take off the masks of pretense. You will tell the truth and there will be an atmosphere of sincerity and openness in your home. All will learn that they are loved unconditionally for who they really are, not the pretenses they show to the world.

IMAGINARY INTERACTION

Imaginary interaction doesn't mean talking to yourself. It's a communication strategy that enables you to anticipate encounters with your children in advance. Through the use of the imagination, parents indirectly experience themselves in anticipated conversations or moments of discipline with their children. This strategy helps you maintain self-control and think more clearly about consequences as well as objections from your children.

There are three primary functions of imagined interaction: increased understanding between yourself and your children (getting your message across), rehearsal (planning for reactions, questions, and objections), and healing (relieving tension). Imagined interactions afford you opportunities to consider (and even mentally envision) the act of talking calmly with your children, to plan their responses, and to better understand and empathize with them.

Imaginary interactions in advance of conflict can be used to reach more satisfactory conclusions. It may also help you avoid falling into the traps of losing your temper, screaming, threatening, or demeaning your children. You can review positive conflict resolution strategies and eliminate negative responses such as physical aggression or criticism.

Parents who try to avoid conflict and the negative emotions that it engenders will have more difficulty engaging in imaginary interactions. With practice, however, you'll be able to use imaginary interactions to achieve greater understanding and to rehearse upcoming actual communication. The imaginary conversation also can be a good opportunity to give yourself mental pep talks: "I can handle this." "I'm not a bad parent." "This isn't the end of the world." "We can find a solution to this problem."

If your three-year-old is having a temper tantrum, you obviously won't have the time to engage in an imaginary conversation. Temper tantrums arrive, like tornadoes in Kansas, unexpected and without warning. While a temper tantrum may leave you babbling to yourself, this is not the same as an imaginary interaction.

Imaginary interactions are more helpful when you're in a situation that's grown out of a conflict with older children. For example, if your teenager is pouting or screaming protests about being grounded for the weekend, you can take the time to walk through an imagined interaction with him. Use this imagined conversation to review the reasons for the discipline, to make sure you're ready to express genuine empathy, and to prepare responses to some of the charges your teenager will probably make. For example, you can anticipate that your teenager will say, "This is so unfair." You can respond with, "You're right. Life can be unfair and I am sure that you feel a grave sense of injustice at this moment. Keep in mind that the grounding is a direct result of your own choice."

If you anticipate that any attempt to communicate with your upset teenager will lead to screaming, prepare yourself to stay calm, keep your voice even, and make sure that you are emotionally prepared to maintain self-control. Remember that the natural response to discipline is for children to complain and argue. When you accept these typical responses in advance, you will be better prepared to walk your children through the painful process of discipline.

In essence, imaginary interactions give you the opportunity to come up with a plan for dealing with angry children and tough interpersonal situations. When you have a plan, you are less likely to explode into ranting and threatening and accusing your children. At a recent workshop, a mom told me, "I know that I just lose it with my daughter. She's twelve years old and when she gets mad at me, she says things that hurt my feelings. Then I just let her have it without thinking." Here is an example of a mom who needs to work through some long-standing issues between her and her daughter. She can benefit from imaginary interaction. If this kind of communication strategy fails to get results, talk with a trusted friend or make an appointment with a family therapist. Whether you talk through conflict alone or with someone else, the very exercise of verbalizing the issues can lead to positive resolution.

You can avoid a lot of traps by engaging in imaginary conversations with your children. Talk your way through the entire problem or situation. In other words, have a dress rehearsal before confronting the misbehavior of your child. You will be calmer, more rational, and less likely to make mistakes. You will be able to anticipate the reactions of your children and you will gain more awareness of yourself and your child. I believe imaginary interactions are a powerful technique for parents.

COMMUNICATE, COMMUNICATE, AND COMMUNICATE

Communication in the same environment and with the same people produces a variety of interpretations, prejudices, assumptions, and beliefs. So much of it is subconscious. These nascent ways of understanding each other can become carved in stone. Family members draw conclusions about each other, but nothing is ever said out loud. The silence covers the pain.

We cannot take back our words, our moods, our feelings, our actions, and our interactions with other people. They're irreversible. We can, however, change their perceptions by changing how we communicate. This is the hard work of genuine efforts at communication. Once our minds are made up and our opinions carved in stone, we have difficulty seeing a person in a different light. No wonder the religious world calls such an experience "repentance." To repent means to think again, literally to have a change of mind. Sometimes our opinions of another person are so ingrained that we pass along those opinions to every generation in our family.

What you say to your children may be perfectly clear to you in terms of your intention. The effect it has on your family may be completely different from your intention. Love and good intentions often stay locked in our hearts. We assume everyone in the family knows. Thus we're not conscious of the blocks that stop our intentions from being understood. Intentions have to be communicated so they can be recognized and understood.

Different goals, motives, and attitudes can clog up family communication. Archie Bunker said, "The reason you don't understand me, Edith, is that I'm talking to you in English and you're listening to me in Dingbat." Communication scholar Gregory Bateson identified and named "complementary schismogenesis"—a mutually aggravating spiral by which each person's response to the other's behavior provokes more exaggerated forms of an unwanted behavior.

A lot of family turmoil can be avoided by good communication. As the primary teacher of your children, make sure you teach communication skills. Remember that intimacy and closeness are essential for your children's healthy emotional development. Allan Gurganus, in *Oldest Living Confederate Widow Tells All,* presents a moving vignette that reminds me of the eternal connection between a parent and his or her children:

You know what a mother's day is like, even with her brood gone? Well, I look at your sweater's nice color and I think, He will like this shade. I eat French toast for breakfast and think, She's crazy for her sweets. Many a pleasure harks on back to them. Might sound strange but fact is, I'm yet looking after their interests. It's almost like they voted for me. Too weak to stay on theirselves, they picked their scrappiest one to tarry here, to keep an eye out for their rights. A dead person still has rights, you know. That's part of why I hang on, stay honest, seek pleasure—it's for what of them is left in me. And, too, for what of me slid off when my kin did. Living or no, we got to represent each other. It's only right. The world is...like the House of Representatives. I keep getting elected to it. I don't even know who's left alive to vote me in. But, child, remember, even sitting here in bed and bent this double, I still stand for them.

For years I struggled to get my son Jeffrey to talk to me. He just never cared much for verbal exercise. Then one morning, I left Jeffrey a note to let him know I was confident he would pass an important math test. What I learned was that Jeffrey appreciated my notes. He saved all my notes in a shoebox in his room. I have left him notes and letters ever since. If you talk to Jeffrey, he will tell you that I now write epistles. But then, when a parent finds something that works, we do tend to wear it out, don't we? Here is one of the letters I sent to Jeffrey:

Dear Son:

I thank God for you as I remember you always in my prayers. I often think of all the times I have encouraged you to stir up that inner fire of ambition, that little spark that lives in your heart, instead of caving in to laziness or apathy or sloth. You have been given a powerful mind and you should never be ashamed of using it for academic success. Keep my words in mind as you start this new semester at school. Embrace the hardships that study and commitment and good grades entail on a daily basis.

Concentrate on being the best possible student. Remember the words of St. Paul to young Timothy: "Study to show yourself a workman with nothing to be ashamed of."

Love, Dad

Sometimes parents have a hard time talking to their children. We know what we feel, we even know what we want to say, but the words won't form in our mouth. Our tongues get heavy and our mind fogs over with confusion. My suggestion is to write out your feelings. Use letters, notes, and poems to express how you feel. I also believe this is an appropriate channel for motivation. Keep the letter short and to the point. Be positive and express your deep caring and love for your child. Encourage and motivate your child.

COMMUNICATE CHARACTER

The theme of this chapter is simple: New times mandate that parents become better communicators than ever before. In my context, a communicator is a persuader. Persuasion, in the context of your family, means using all the means at your disposal to convince your children that you have their best interests at heart. You teach them the basic values that will help them become mature, independent human beings.

The information explosion has played a central role in changing the way our children receive and understand our appeals. The persuasive appeals of our culture are so much more sophisticated. Our children are bombarded with so many claims. How do we get our children to listen to us when so many negative messages are packaged so irresistibly? You can't shield your children from every perceived harm. I believe a more appropriate response is for you to become a more effective persuader.

As Aristotle taught us centuries earlier, the power to persuade depends on character, reason, and emotions. I believe that character is the essential element in a parent's ability to be a persuader. It represents who you are, what you believe in, and how you embody those values. Of course, the evaluation of character is a highly subjective notion, and children are not well equipped in this area. Your character, after all, is always filtered through your children's perceptions. It's no coincidence that children frequently refer to their parents as "hypocrites."

How do you communicate character to your children? First ask, What is your message to your children? You have to have a focused, central message that describes your understanding of life. Just as a CEO might have a mission statement that describes what the company stands for, your message describes your family's values and goals. Your job is to communicate that message to your kids and embody it in your character. For example, my central message to my children is: "Life is a gift. Life as it is given is good. Therefore in all the ups and downs of living, we will look for the good and work for the common good. We will not allow despair or cynicism to put a chip on our shoulder and bring us down." I work hard to embody these goals in how I live, and I remind our children of these values often.

Your life forms a long prelude to your message. How your children interpret what you say or do may not be clear or correct. Your daily experiences with your children are the building blocks of parental character. Your character is a constructed reality. It's not an essence, waiting to be truthfully revealed; rather, a particular family in a specific persuasive context actively constructs it. Your children, in very specific daily contexts and encounters, actively, daily, continuously construct your character. They'll make varying evaluations of your character as a parent. They'll decide if you are kind or mean, good or bad, a truth teller or a liar. They'll conclude they're loved or hated, accepted or rejected. What this means is that you need to check your actions and statements constantly to be sure you're embodying character that's consistent with your message.

Parents gain authority through a consistent, loving, teaching, caring character. Through your character, you can win your children to a particular way of living. For example, children need to be converted to a life of responsibility—a life that's well ordered, meaningful, and joyful. This can only happen when you are clear about your own interests and purposes. What are you saying, teaching, and doing?

I have communicated character in my family by trying to be consistent with my teaching and my action. For example, I have taught my children the importance of honesty. I act in honest ways toward others. The teller at the supermarket gave me twenty dollars too much in change. I handed the money to my daughter Melissa and said, "She gave me back too much money. What should we do?" Melissa handed the twenty-dollar-bill back to the cashier. If you want honesty to be a family value, model honesty. If you want to raise responsible kids, model responsibility and give them choices to develop their own.

Here is a representative sample of the kind of values I taught my children:

1. Work hard. There is no free ride.
2. Set goals: short-term and long-term. Learn how to reach your goals one at a time.
3. Don't do the least you can to get by.
4. Think for yourself.
5. Learn to solve problems without crying, whining, or blaming.
6. Find something constructive to do.
7. Always do your best.
8. Never give up.
9. Know what you believe about life.
10. Have a purpose.
11. Study hard and do well in school.
12. Be a friend and make friends.
13. Treat all people with respect.

What is your message, and what are your values? Take some time to make your own list.

COMMUNICATE LOVE

Love and acceptance are essential for healthy child development, to building feelings of self-worth and self-esteem. Affection is the most crucial of all the influences provided in the home. If we get this part right, we're already 80 percent successful as parents. When you give your child affection and acceptance, you establish a sense of trust that helps him or her deal with fear and anxiety.

How do you communicate love in your family? First, make time for your children to express their experiences, feelings, and needs. Listening is love in action. Second, make sure your communication is positive, not negative. Notice and acknowledge what your child does right, and put less emphasis on what he does wrong. You'll be amazed at how much more motivated and embraced kids feel by such positive reinforcement. Third, offer affection nonverbally through touch. Kids need lots of smiles, hugs, and kisses.

Some parents fall into the trap of taking for granted that their children know they're loved. In an episode of *Frazier,* Niles and Frazier go ice fishing with their dad. Neither of them cares anything about ice fishing. In fact, the very idea of these two city slickers on a frozen lake fishing is absurd. They go ice fishing because they're desperate for their dad to tell them, "I love you." The story rings true to the audience because so many people have parents who loved them but never got around to saying those magic words. When we take love for granted, it can be a short slide to ignoring or avoiding the children, using sarcasm or negative and critical comments, or creating physical distance from them. Children then begin to feel low self-esteem, feelings of inadequacy or insecurity, increased aggression, loneliness, generalized fear or anxiety, and difficulties in both the giving and receiving of love. Look for opportunities to tell your kids as often as you can, "I love you."

Families that communicate love encourage children's competence and self-confidence. The rewards come not just in cognitive matters such as reading, writing, and speaking, but in our children's capacity to care about others, deal with their feelings, and respond to stress. When we show our love, we communicate the highest part of our character.

CHAPTER 7

TEACHING ROUTINES

THE NUMBER-ONE PROBLEM faced by parents isn't discipline; it's the lack of routines and daily habits. A vast majority of children's behavior problems happen because they haven't been taught to follow routines. A chaotic home environment is usually the result of disorganization, distractions, and a helter-skelter approach to parenting. Children are confused because the only constant in their lives is change. Every day, they and their parents seem to wake up in a new world. The rules are inconsistent, unspoken, or made up on the spur of the moment. The result of all this chaos is usually frayed nerves, exhaustion, and anger. You can eliminate the majority of discipline problems by establishing basic routines.

I have learned the value of routines from a variety of sources. Football coaches know the value of routines. The coach has his team run the same plays over and over in practice. Players get tired of repeating the same play day after day. Then, on game night, a young 137-pound wide receiver goes out for a pass over the middle and gets run over by a large bus. In a semiconscious state, the little receiver stumbles back to the huddle. He's looking out of the earhole of his helmet and eating grass for dinner. The quarterback calls the play the team has been running over and over in practice. The receiver goes out 15 yards, plants his foot, and cuts toward the sideline. He catches the pass for a first down. Routines are powerful.

These are the main reasons why children don't follow routines:

1. The parent hasn't thought out what happens in the home every day. Instead, rules are constantly shifting. Mom and Dad are not on the same page when deciding how things are going to be at home.

2. The children have not been taught to follow the routines. Often parents have a pretty clear idea of their way of doing things, but they fail to communicate the routines to the children. In other words, they make the false assumption that their children will automatically understand. Please never live under the illusion that your children somehow possess the automatic ability to read your mind. You need to spell it out over and over. Repetition is the heart of good parenting.

3. The parent spends no time managing the children. Many parents live as if there are no children on the premises. Everyone in the family is on his or her own. The only commonality in such families is the shared living space. Otherwise the children are coming and going without much or any communication. Many homes have no one in particular in charge. At times the children are in charge. When chaos reaches a fever pitch, one of the parents has a temper tantrum and takes charge for a small amount of time. The resulting coercion throws the family into more emotional distress and confusion.

The majority of the crises in the home are caused by the failure of parents to have routines or the failure of children to follow routines. Obviously if the children don't know the routines, they can't follow them. Routines concern how things are done. "This is the way we go to school. This is the way we eat our meals. This is the way we take our baths. This is the way we go to bed." Routines become habits and as we know from experience, habits are carried out without whining, crying, complaining, or blaming others.

I've learned so much about the value of routines by observing the classrooms of outstanding teachers. Great teachers have almost no discipline problems. When I tried to figure out why such teachers had well-constructed, well-managed classrooms, I discovered that they all had one thing in common: a set of routines that are taught and implemented every day.

Johnelle's middle school was originally designed to be a kindergarten-through-second-grade building. Small halls for small people. The present occupants, middle school boys and girls, were having trouble changing classes. They were bumping into one another when they went to their lockers. The halls were crowded and kids were getting frustrated and angry. To deal with this potential discipline problem, Johnelle called a general assembly. The entire student body gathered in the gym. During this session, Johnelle explained the new routine for changing classes. Step by step, she went over how she wanted her students to move from class to class between each period. For the boys she devised a little song for them to repeat as a reminder of the routine: "Move to the right, keep my hands to myself, and pull up my pants." The "pull up the pants" referred to those wide-butt blue jeans the boys wore to school which were always threatening to slide off their hips. After one week, the new routine had settled down the entire student body. Almost six hundred middle school kids moved quietly from class to class without arguments, conflicts, or fights.

Routines save time and energy. The equation works like this. The more routines you have and teach to your children, the fewer discipline problems you will experience. In the beginning, all the time spent teaching routines may seem redundant and even boring. It's a lot of hard work and drudgery, and the temptation to let things slide is huge. The reward, however, comes when your children have settled into the routine and accepted your way of doing things at home. There will be other special rewards: less confusion, a quieter home, a more peaceful home, fewer arguments, and fewer distractions. Your home will operate like a well-drilled basketball team. You will be happier. There will be less stress in your life.

Don't blame your children if your home environment is out of control when there are no regular routines to guide behavior and action. Children can be taught to accept the idea of having a consistent set of family routines because it makes life easier and simpler for everyone. You will be able to go about your business or pleasure without having to stop every few minutes to referee fights or "micromanage" your children. If there are no routines, a lot of negative energy goes into explaining and arguing and making children behave. The lack of routines also leads to children acquiring bad work habits and behaviors that are hard to correct.

What I'm suggesting can be called preventive discipline. Being a parent takes a lot of time and energy. If you expend your time and energy teaching routines, you will be working in a positive and healthy way. If you spend your time and energy dispensing discipline, you will be working in a negative and unhealthy way. Constant attention to negative discipline disrupts the smoothness of family life. That kind of discipline only brings a temporary halt to bad behavior. A parent who spends most of his or her time in discipline is wasting time.

Children don't learn many positive lessons from negative discipline. There is so much negative energy—everyone accuses and blames everyone else. The result is an unhealthy family environment. Since you have to invest time and energy raising children, wouldn't you rather use that time and energy in positive teaching rather than in negative discipline? The reasons coaches have their players repeat the same plays over and over again is that the more they run the plays, the more of a routine habit the plays become, and the better they'll be able to execute the plays during the game. The reason a golfer practices every day is that the more he practices, the better golfer he becomes.

Effective teachers know that the more time spent on task by the student, the more the student learns.

Routines allow the family to live together smoothly. My first parenting workbook was called *When Is this Place Gonna Get Smooth?* A smooth-running home is free of confusion and is a pleasure to live in.

THE VALUE OF ROUTINES

Routines are essential in our culture. They enable people to get along in acceptable orderly ways. Daily life is made up of ordinary routines that help us make sense of our work, our leisure, our worship, and our lives. Three or four times a week, for example, I board an airplane for a flight to a parenting workshop somewhere in the world. After the cabin door has been shut and secured, the flight attendant explains the procedures. I have heard these procedures so many times that I can chant them along with the attendant. More important, these procedures have become a part of my own daily flight routine. I only give cursory attention to the instructions about the seat belt, the oxygen mask, and the flotation device under my seat cushion, and the red lights along the aisle that will guide me to the appropriate exit. Without whining, crying, or complaining, I fasten my seat belt, remain in my seat while the seat belt light is on, and refrain from hassling the flight attendant. These procedures help our flight go smoothly and enable the attendants to do their jobs effectively.

When a person doesn't know the local customs, ways, or traditions, there is a lot of confusion and misunderstanding. To get along with other people, it's necessary to know the local ways of doing things. When I give a cultural diversity workshop, I divide my audience into ten groups of four persons each. At each table, I place a deck of cards. I instruct the group that we're going to play cards for the next thirty minutes. Written instructions and rules are distributed to each group. Everyone has five minutes to read over the rules. The group is told that once the game begins, no talking will be allowed. At the end of each round of card games, the winner at each table moves to his or her right and plays the next round at a new table. The loser at each table moves to his or her left and plays the next round at that table. This continues until the 30-minute time limit is reached.

The players don't know that each table has been given a different set of rules. As the exercise unfolds, the players become frustrated, agitated, defensive, aggressive, argumentative. There is chaos as the winner at a previous game reaches to capture a trick he thinks he has won and another player slaps his hand and takes the trick. At some tables, a referee is needed to calm down the players and remind them that no talking is allowed.

At the end of the exercise, we talk and unpack the experience. Someone complains that the rules were unfair. Another participant says the rules were not clear. Finally, someone says the rules were different at every table. Continuing to process the emotions generated by the game, we discover that we have all been in new places where we didn't know the rules or the routines or the way that we were expected to behave.

Participants complete the exercise with a new awareness of how essential routines are in enabling us to function in acceptable and organized ways. Your children are strangers in a strange land. They don't know the local customs and rules. Every time you want something done in a certain way, you have to teach them a routine or a set of routines.

Routines answer such questions as these:

- What to do about family chores
- What to do when there is a disagreement
- What to do when Mom says "It's time for bed"
- What to do when the alarm sounds to get up for school
- What to do about homework
- What to do when you have questions and Mom or Dad is busy
- What to do at the dinner table
- What to do when you want to do something

A routine is how you want something done; it's your responsibility to make sure the routine is clearly understood.

REPEAT, REPEAT, REPEAT

The lessons have to be repeated. By the way, did I tell you that the lessons have to be repeated? Children don't get the point or understand the lesson simply because their parent tells them one time. So cut them some slack and realize that kids will be kids. They're not trying to be mean or bad or outrageous. They just don't get the point yet. So repeat the lessons and do so with patience and kindness and gentleness.

One of our children bought a Dodge Dakota Sport pickup truck. We had a long discussion about the insurance requirements. "Nobody else is allowed to drive your truck. Do you understand?" "Yes," he said. Two weeks later, he let his girlfriend drive his truck. She had a wreck; the police decided it was her fault. The cost for repairing our son's truck was $850. He couldn't afford to make a claim on his insurance because the company would have raised his rates too high for him to afford the payments. I told him he would have to drive the truck the way it was. His girlfriend's mother paid the $850 and he was happy.

Three months later, our son let his college roommate drive the Dakota. Another accident, another bill. Obviously, the lesson hadn't sunk in. This time he ate the cost. A motivating natural consequence.

How many children are reading on a twelfth-grade level and whining on a first-grade level? Emotional maturity and intellectual development are not equal to each other. Knowledge doesn't equate to wisdom. Even a very smart teenager is quite capable of having temper tantrums, whining, complaining, blaming, and fighting. Repeating the lessons of a routine with patience and gentleness will help your child accept responsibility. Make sure you set the routines, not your kids.

Parents who mistake knowledge for maturity have a tendency to "ask" their children to do things. They discuss everything and let the child basically run the household. I hear parents ask their children, "Where would you like to eat dinner?" not as an occasional experience but as an everyday question. Smart children are often in charge at home. Their parents are so sensitive to the children's needs, so caught up in their intelligence that they forget how much direction, guidance, and discipline all children need. Learning to get along with others is an important part of a child's education. Learning the meaning of delayed gratification is just as essential. There is no reason under the sun to spoil a child simply because you're impressed with his or her intelligence. Revel in your children's intelligence, but make sure you give them the emotional support they need. And make sure that you provide the structure, consistency, and firm discipline that's required for a well-balanced childhood. Routines will help.

Do the right thing even when you don't get immediate, right results. The consistency of your approach and the cumulative effect of your discipline will pay off in better behavior by your children. Evaluate results of any particular discipline over a long period of time. For example, instead of trying for two nights to get your child to bed on time then giving up, dedicate yourself to trying for as many nights as necessary to achieve the desired results. You'll be better served spending thirty nights getting your child to bed. Otherwise you're in for years of difficulty, fighting, whining, and losing battles. Besides, who wants a nine-year-old sleeping in the same bed with them?

Adults become too easily frustrated by the immature behavior of children. Remember, the keys are consistency and cumulative effects. Hang in there and keep at the routine. It'll be the best two weeks you'll ever invest. Your children will come around to your point of view with time and patience. Keep in mind that they feed off your negative emotional energy. That's how you maintain the climate in your home. The warm water of the Gulf of Mexico provides the necessary ingredients for a hurricane to grow larger and more destructive. Our children come flying across our adult terrain like little tropical storms. If we're out of control, if we toss routines aside, the storm will grow larger and meaner and more destructive. You're the weather maker in your home. You set the climate. You control the environment.

There are three steps to teaching routines.

1. *Teach.* After deciding what routines you're going to use, teach your children how to carry out the routine. You can demonstrate and tell them what you expect.

2. *Repeat at least fourteen times.* You should repeat the routine every day for fourteen straight days, longer if necessary. That's how long it'll take to make a routine second nature.

3. *Reteach and reinforce.* From time to time, go back over the routine and reinforce its importance in the lives of your children.

Start by making a list of all the routines you need to establish for all the areas of family life that are now war zones. These occur generally first thing in the morning before school or at the end of the day before bed. For each routine, make a list of specific requirements. The clearer your expectations, the easier it will be for your kids to follow them. For example, instead of listing "Get ready for school" as your morning routine, you might want to list:

The Morning Routine

1. Be downstairs, fully dressed, with socks and shoes on and hair brushed, before 7:30.
2. When you're through eating, put breakfast dishes in sink.
3. Pack up lunch and/or school snack.
4. Wash face, brush teeth, and make bed.
5. Double-check backpack.
6. Be on the bus corner by 8:15.

If you're spelling out a nighttime routine, you might want a list that looks something like this:

Before Bed

1. Put dirty clothes in hamper
2. Pack up backpack with completed homework; make sure any school notes are signed or school announcements given to parents.

3. Lay out clothes for the next day.
4. Pick up toys, put away games and puzzles.
5. Brush teeth and wash face.
6. Read for 20 minutes.

The more specific your list is, the less chaotic things will be. The "Before Bed" list above came from one of the parents I know, who always found her mornings with her kids so frantic. Tempers would rise as kids dribbled downstairs half-dressed, homework missing or half-done, clamoring for last-minute signatures or money for a class trip. Breakfast would sit uneaten as kids raced around, tearfully trying to find missing shoes or jackets. As the minutes ticked toward the appointed arrival of the bus, this mother found herself screaming at her kids and they responded by screaming right back. "Why didn't you tell me you needed a shoebox for a class project?" "It's not my fault, I forgot to check my backpack!" She'd always envisioned herself sending her kids off to school with a warm hug and a whispered "I love you." Now she was sending them off with mutually resentful looks. Then she switched to creating routines. She went through the hard work of teaching her kids to follow them. Within two weeks, mornings became peaceful, unrushed gatherings. Even the kids agreed this was so much better, and that motivated them to stick to the routines.

Your list needs to be as clear as possible. I think we all know that our idea of "clean" isn't the same as our kids'. If your routine is "Clean your room," give each child a specific list that fits his age, ability, and room. Toddlers as young as three can be told, "A clean room is a room where your dirty clothes are in the hamper, your trucks are on the shelf, your toys go in the toy box, and your stuffed animals go on the rocking chair." An older child might be told, "A clean room is a room where your LEGOs are stowed under your bed, your desktop is free of clutter, your clothes are all put away, and your books are on the shelves." Or, "A clean room is a room where I can have a free path to your bed." Your definition of clean won't be the same as everyone else's. What's important is that you communicate it to your child.

Once you've created your lists, have a family meeting and review them. Make sure each child understands what's expected of him or her. Answer questions and revise the list as necessary. Tell the kids that these routines will make everyone's life easier. They need to know that learning a routine is always bumpy at first. It takes longer to do things, everyone will need a lot of reminding, mistakes will be made. But if the whole family sticks with the routine, it'll become second nature and things will get done much more quickly. Post the lists in your children's rooms. Some parents also post a copy on the refrigerator or near the breakfast table for easy reminders.

A written list has another advantage: It becomes the focal point for your child, not your reminders. For the first week or two, you will be giving constant, specific reminders, but let the list do most of the dirty work. "Did you do your morning routine? Check your list." Or "Did you do your bedtime routine? No playing until you finish everything on the list."

Establish consequences for not following the routine; you can either decide these yourself or let your kids offer suggestions. One mom who found herself constantly ferrying forgotten sneakers, band instruments, and homework to school for her kids established a routine that included having her kids pack up their backpacks the night before. She then told them, "If you don't pack up your backpacks, you have your pick of two consequences. One consequence is you take your lumps at school; getting marked down in gym because you didn't bring your sneakers or in band because you didn't bring your trumpet. The other consequence is that if you want to call to hire Mom's Taxi Service to bring this stuff to school for you, it'll cost you three dollars." The family agreed they would put the taxi service money into a charity jar to be donated every month to the charity of their choice.

Try to relate consequences as naturally as you can. For example, if your child's routine includes doing homework as soon as she gets home from school and she blows it off, a natural consequence would be no playdates for a day or two so she doesn't have the distraction of the playdate to keep her from her homework. Some parents establish some variant of "toy jail," where any toys not put away at the appointed time have to live for a certain amount of time before they're returned to the child.

Let's look at some more examples of routines.

Routine for the End of the Day

We call our end-of-the-day routine, "wind-down" time. Thirty minutes before bedtime, I announce, "It's wind-down time." That means that our children have thirty minutes to spend in their own room. They have permission to do whatever they want as long as they're quiet. After thirty minutes, Johnelle and I spend about fifteen minutes in each child's room and put the closing touches on the day. Reading, conversation, a review of the day's events and experiences, and prayers are our routine practices. Then we turn out the light, say "Good night," and leave the room. We don't use a threatening, ominous voice that demands, "Now, you better go to sleep or else." Those words aren't exactly conducive to a good night's sleep. After all, how can you make a child go to sleep? Are you going to staple their eyes shut?

If your child gets into the habit of popping out of bed numerous times, you simply add a rule to your routine. For example, tell your child, "You may get up one time after going to bed. If you get up more than once, you won't be allowed to watch television tomorrow evening." Or you might say, "The rule is no getting out of bed for water, snacks, or questions. If you get up, you will not get to play outside tomorrow." If your child ignores the warning and the consequence, you keep putting him or her back in the bed until the message is clear—you expect him or her to stay in the bed. Maintain your cool. Be firm. With a few nights of consistent preventive discipline on your part, your children will learn that you mean what you say. Whatever you do, don't panic and turn the situation into a war. Use your best judgment about your child's getting up to ask a question or get a drink of water. You can tell if your child is making a legitimate, one-time request or trying to take charge.

Routine for Meals

If your family meals are filled with stress, arguments, fights, and chaos, you need a mealtime routine. At a recent seminar, a mother asked me for help with a problem at meals. She and her husband have four children. All of them are under the age of eight. Her husband has very strict rules about eating and spends every meal arguing and lecturing the children about proper table manners. The result is confusion and chaos. No one is enjoying the family meal. I suggested that the family have two formal meals each month. The family can pull out all the best china, silver, and crystal and they can eat in the most ignored of rooms—the dining room. Then the husband can use his teaching expertise to point out proper table manners. The other family meals can then be more informal and relaxed occasions where the family enjoys being with one another.

The mealtime routine we use is very simple. If one of the children doesn't wish to eat with the family and causes disruptions at the table, we put the child's plate in the refrigerator and excuse the child from the table. Our misbehaving child is sent to his or her room and stays there until hunger brings him or her back. When the child returns later, after we've finished dinner, and asks for something to eat, we tell him or her that the food is in the refrigerator. The child, if he or she is old enough, warms the food in the microwave and then sits at the table and eats alone. The message we are sending is, "Family meals are peaceful. You are welcome back when you can be peaceful."

Parents frequently ask me for help with food-related battles. "My child won't eat." "He won't sit at the table without causing trouble." "She whines and complains that the food tastes bad." Once again, you want to avoid the invitation to battle. You can make sure there is one thing on your child's plate that you know he or she will eat. You can provide plenty of healthy fruits and vegetables for your children's snacks. The issue probably isn't your fear that your child will starve, it's that you want a peaceful meal. Your message should be, "We don't give in to whining or temper tantrums. If you can't sit at the table peacefully, you'll have to leave."

Instead of turning meals into emotional disasters, maintain your calm and do everything possible to make the experience positive and joyous. Once your child realizes that fighting over food is a waste of time, calm will return to your family meal.

Routine for Completing Chores

For a child to experience wholeness, there needs to be a healthy balance between chores and play. "All work and no play makes Johnny a dull boy" may sound like a cliché, but it's still valid. Some parents consider work a necessary evil. These parents only do what has to be done and tend to teach their children the same laissez-faire philosophy. A hard-nosed, no-nonsense parent may view play as unnecessary. The sense of balance that I'm looking for values both work and play.

Chores at an early age set the groundwork for a child's experiences with homework. A child who has been taught how to work hard, how to set and reach goals is more likely to succeed with homework. I realize that getting kids to do chores can be a tough sell for parents. You have a couple of options available. You can complain and whine about household chores and demand that your children do their fair share of the work around the house. Or you can present chores in a positive light and let the children know that you both need and welcome their help. Work can be fun.

Even those ordinary chores that have to be repeated daily can become a part of the natural rhythms of family life. You can help your children learn that housework and chores are "unfinished business" all the time. Dishes get dirty and have to be washed every night. The grass has to be mowed every week during the mowing season. In Louisiana, where I live, that's every month except January and part of February. Cloths have to be washed and dried so we have something clean to wear tomorrow. The floor has to be swept, mopped, waxed, or vacuumed. Beds have to be made.

Johnelle hates to come home from work and find an unmade bed. So we taught our children to make their own bed each morning before leaving for school. The task is fairly simple and doesn't take but a few moments. Show and tell children the details of making the bed and move on to the next chore.

Never cheat children out of the joy of learning to work hard. The everyday chores in a family are essential to our well-being as well as our daily existence. Borrow from the meditation tradition of some of the world's great traditions and teach children that work is "love made visible." High spiritual value is accorded to the simplest of tasks. The "everydayness of every day" is celebrated. Doing work that has to be done over and over again puts us in touch with the realities of the cycles of nature.

My own mother made our summer chores of shelling and canning peas as much fun as possible. We usually shelled bushel baskets of purple hull peas in large family groups. We laughed and talked and took breaks to play ball. But we shelled a lot of peas. These fresh vegetables tasted very good in the cold, short days of December. There was a sense of real accomplishment about helping the family put food on the table.

I believe that chores are essential for children. They help children recognize the joy of the "everdayness of every day." Chores also help children

- Develop the ability to organize their time and resources
- Experience the rewards of a job well done
- Organize their tasks into small and reachable goals
- Learn how to solve problems
- Prepare for the more difficult work assignments of their adult lives.

We approach chores as teamwork. Our children know that they're members of "The Kennedy Team." In order for our family to thrive, we need everyone's help.

Encourage children's participation in family work with these positive communications:

- "You're an important member of our team."
- "We need your help or we will never get all the work done around here."
- "We're counting on you."
- "You make a real contribution to the family."
- "You make us so proud because of the way you help out without being asked."

- "Thanks for helping with the chores."
- "I appreciate your hard work around the house."
- "The yard looks really great this week."

Chores need to start early. Remember, there is a magical age when children are constantly begging to help. Take full advantage of this fleeting period of altruism. In our family, at age three you got to take the little trash cans from the bathrooms and put them in the kitchen next to the big trash can. At four you got to help unload the dishwasher and help set the table. At five you could make your own bed. By ten you could wash and dry your own clothes and help with the yard work.

The magical moment will expire and kids will catch on that work isn't always complete fun. But by that time, the routines of your family will be firmly set. Remember that chores are the nuts and bolts of your long-term parenting goal. You want your children to be independent when they leave home. In order to reach that goal, you will want to teach them how to take care of themselves and do everything for themselves.

Make a list of everything you're presently doing for your children. What are you doing that you can let the children do? Don't worry that it takes longer to teach them a chore than to do it yourself. Forget that they probably won't complete the chore to your satisfaction. They won't do it as fast as or well as you would. But remember the big advantage: *You're not doing the chore.* And you're investing in raising a responsible child.

What about paying children to do the chores? Bribes and rewards appear to be an easy way to motivate children to help out at home. But is this a good approach? I don't think so. One of my sons asked me to pay him $40 to mow the grass every week. Instead of agreeing to the deal, I asked him to help me do a little math lesson. "Son, I already pay you a lot. Let's see. I let you live in my house, use my air conditioning, drive my car, eat my food, and use my credit card. I feed you, clothe you, and shelter you. According to these calculations you're already making eighty dollars an hour to mow the lawn. That's even better than union scale." He understood, but that didn't prevent him from griping some.

What happens when your child just doesn't want to do chores? Please. You're surely strong enough to push past this lame excuse. The important lesson isn't whether the child really likes doing the chore, but that the chore is completed and the satisfaction of a job well done is reward enough. Again you have to keep the long-range goal in mind and not fall for the temporary discomfort of an unhappy child. Protesting that he doesn't like the chore is a good opportunity to teach a lesson. "Life is full of ordinary tasks that we complete every day in order to experience a greater satisfaction." Whether children like chores or not is irrelevant in the long run. What matters is that you motivate them to do their work and supervise its successful conclusion.

When Kirkland was four, his main chore was bringing the small trash containers to the utility room. On Saturday morning, long after the chores were supposed to be finished, we found him sitting in the chaise lounge reading a book. Johnelle said, "Kirkland, you didn't finish your chores." At the time, she was using a discipline system that included a chart where she marked misbehavior with an X. Kirkland looked up from his book and said, "I know. I think I'll just take an X today." Ingenious response? No doubt. Creative answer for a four-year-old? Of course. But the chores still needed to be finished. So Johnelle gave Kirkland a simple discipline of not playing with his favorite toy for the rest of the day and got him out of the chaise lounge to do his chores.

For younger, balkier kids, you will need a mountain of practice.

One of the important first steps is letting your two- and three-year-old children help you. Children usually are underfoot at these ages and always want to help. At this stage in their development, don't worry about competence. Allow your kids to do what they can, along with you. They'll learn that chores are what we do to keep the household running.

You can also discuss family chores with your children. I don't believe it's necessary to order children around. Each week, you can allow one of your children to chair the "Chores Committee." You can allow the chairperson to allocate the chores. It's also important to vary the chores that each child does. When you give one of your children a new chore, make sure you spend time teaching him or her how to do it to your satisfaction. There will be times when you'll need to pitch in and help your child get the chore finished. The important principle is always the same: Refuse to be lured into making chores, or meals, or bedtime a battle.

Maintain a positive attitude toward work and chores. Your children are more likely to catch your attitude and form opinions about work based on their observations of you. It's okay to express understanding when children complain about chores; just keep it positive. "I know you're tired, but I really appreciate your help." "Thanks for getting the trash out to the street tonight. It's a hassle to wait until the morning." Complaints are not indicators that children don't do their chores. Complaints are a mechanism for expressing dissatisfaction. Don't take them too seriously.

To help myself maintain a consistent approach to chores, I use the three Cs:

- *Chores:* The family decides together on the weekly allocation of chores. Everyone has responsibilities for helping out.

- *Choices:* The children choose to complete chores or experience the consequences. By the way, part of the consequences is that the chore still has to be finished.
- *Consequences:* The family agrees on a limited number of simple, practical, and meaningful consequences for failure to complete chores.

I believe that you will have more success in the area of chores by establishing a consistent pattern that you use week after week. Here's an example of a pattern for chores.

1. Assign each child a reasonable number of chores.
2. When your child is assigned a new chore, take as much time as needed to teach him or her how to do the chore. Your goal is reasonable competence not perfection.
3. Expect all chores to be completed within a specific time frame. Your children are more likely to ignore general instructions. Be specific: "Your chores must be completed before seven P.M." "The trash must be taken out every Monday and Thursday." "You have to empty the dishwasher before you go to school."
4. Review assigned chores and proposed consequences. Always attach your consequences to the chores in advance. Your children then know the boundaries, and your expectations are clear.
5. Praise completed chores.
6. Discipline failure to finish chores with the predetermined consequences.
7. If your child is having difficulty with his or her chore, take the time to re-teach the skill needed in this particular area.
8. Vary your child's chores. As part of my children's "voca-

tional education," I give them cross-training in all areas of family work—dishwasher, garbage disposal, washing machine, dryer, lawn mower, leaf blower, edger, weed-eater, cooking utensils, egg poacher, coffee machine, juicer, vacuum, broom, mop, oven, microwave, bread maker, microwave, trash compactor, water hose, and outdoor grill.

9. Whatever you do, never give in to frustration and do all the work for yourself. Keep working on your delegating skills. I'm sure that you have excellent middle-management skills.

What if children still refuse to do their chores? Stand your ground, express your sense of understanding, and expect the chores to be done. For example, my son Jeffrey didn't want to cut the grass. One day he announced, "I'm never cutting your grass again." What an interesting concept: "your grass." Well, I decided to give Jeffrey a choice between his chore of cutting the grass and the consequence of not cutting the grass.

Without raising my voice, I looked right in Jeffrey's eyes and said, "I want you to cut the grass every week before five P.M. every Friday, or you will spend the entire weekend at home with me. Let me know what you decide." Jeffrey had all week to finish the task of caring for the lawn. Here was a piece of creative discipline that didn't involve the loss of dignity on my part or Jeffrey's part.

Although Jeffrey was seventeen years old, he was still somewhat of a kindergartner in the sense of show and tell. Having told him the deal, it now became necessary to show him that I meant business. On the very first Friday, I came home from work at 5:30 P.M. and Jeffrey had not cut the grass. The rain poured down. I could feel my grass growing. I was not a happy dad. On the way into the house, I bumped into Jeffrey.

"Excuse me," I said, "but aren't you forgetting something?"

"No way," he scowled back. "It's Friday. I have money. I'm out of here."

"You didn't cut the grass."

"Man, I can't cut the grass. It's raining outside."

"I understand how you feel, but a deal is a deal. I don't want you cutting grass in the rain. What is important here is that you failed to complete your chore by the agreed deadline. You had all week to cut the grass, but you waited until the last minute and the rain spoiled your chances. You didn't cut the grass and you will have to stay home all weekend."

Jeffrey was really upset. He took the keys out of his pocket and slammed them down on the table. This was his personal invitation to battle. He was asking me to sacrifice my own sense of self-control and fight with him over the consequences of his refusal to cut the grass. Instead I smiled, picked up the keys, and walked out of the kitchen.

Jeffrey stomped upstairs to his room. He slammed the door, turned his music up very loud, and spent the rest of the evening pouting in his room. That was acceptable to me. I never interrupt the sulking of a child. Even though Jeffrey skipped dinner, I didn't go upstairs to check on him. He needed time to reflect upon the seriousness of the choice he'd made.

Early Saturday morning, I got Jeffrey up so he could cut the grass. To ignore the still undone chore would have given him the impression that he really could get away with not cutting the grass. So I got my newspaper, a hot cup of Community dark roast coffee, and took a seat on the patio to watch Jeffrey cut the grass. He finished the task as fast as he could move. Then he wanted to know if he could go out. The answer, of course, was "No." At my parenting workshops, I ask parents if Jeffrey should have been allowed to go out on Saturday evening after finishing his chore. They always answer in unison, "No!" I remind them of how easy it is to parent other people's children! We often know what to do, but we lack the courage or the backbone or the strength of character to carry out the necessary discipline.

The important factor to keep in mind: Children should receive real, practical, and meaningful consequences for failing to finish their chores. When your child doesn't pick up his toys, he will lose the privilege of playing with those toys for the rest of the week. When your child chooses to violate the preset curfew of midnight, he shouldn't be allowed to go out next weekend. If your child goes outside on a rainy day without her raincoat or an umbrella, allow her to experience the natural consequence of getting wet. If your child plays on the school basketball team and makes unacceptable grades, he or she sits out a few games until you and the teacher feel the child is back on track. Chores, choices, and consequences are closely linked in a parent's daily experience.

Go ahead and call me obsessive-compulsive, but from where I sit, in the den of a beautifully decorated home, a messy house isn't an option. Everyone helps keep the house clean. A messy house gets a family out of its daily routines. That doesn't imply that a house has to pass the white glove test or receive the Good Housekeeping seal of approval. I'm not suggesting that your children should be afraid to sit on the furniture in your living room. You should, however, spend time teaching your children how to put things back where they belong. A few simple rules will suffice:

- Keep the pathways through the house uncluttered. Nothing hurts worse than stepping barefooted on a toy in the pitch darkness.
- No dirty dishes in the sink or on the counter. It doesn't take

any more time to put the dishes in the dishwater than it does to leave them on the counter or in the sink.

- Nothing left on the breakfast room table. Every afternoon when we come home from work, the breakfast table is the first thing we see. And we want it clean. No clutter.

- Clean up your own mess.

- Keep the bathroom clean. For a boy that means remembering to raise and lower the lid.

- Don't leave water on the floor after taking a shower.

- Make up the bed every morning. For some reason I have always hated making the bed. Some days, when Johnelle left for work before I got out of bed, I would sneak out and leave the bed unmade. Then I made sure I was home early enough to make the bed before she came home. But gradually she helped me understand that an unmade bed was an emotional distraction to face at the end of a long day of work. With so much chaos in daily life, I try to give some order to our corner of the world. So we each make our own bed every day. We do, however, have permission to skip Saturday morning.

Chores are the contributions each member of the family makes to the team effort. We don't pay our children to do the chores. We expect them to help. Money for chores sends the wrong message.

Again helping out at home is expected, but it still deserves praise when completed. Be an encouraging parent. Tell your kids: "Thank you." "Good job." Never rob your children of the privilege of working hard. There is no free ride. If you worry that children won't like doing chores, put your mind at ease. They'll soon learn that work isn't always fun and games. This is a lesson that needs to be learned early in life. If we only did what we liked, not much would get done.

When our children graduate from college, we're sure they'll want to put a footnote on their resume: *"Trust me, I know how to work hard."* I've heard that corporations pay good money for young men and women with a strong work ethic. And the right place to start is with the teaching of routines.

CHAPTER 8

TEACHING KIDS TO GET ALONG

"CIRCLE THE WAGONS." "FIRE ONE!" Do you ever feel like putting a warning sign in your front yard? *WARNING: YOU'RE ENTERING A COMBAT ZONE.* Parents often act surprised that their children have a hard time getting along with each other. The truth is much simpler. Kids argue, disagree, and fight. I get more questions about sibling rivalry than any other subject at my workshops. Sometimes I think parents forget that conflict is a natural part of life. The question isn't "Will there be conflict in our family?" but "How will we handle conflict in our family?"

As a parent, my goals in teaching conflict resolutions skills are to help my kids

1. Develop positive self-confidence.
2. Tell the difference between feelings and actions.
3. Celebrate the diversity of various individual and groups who make up the school, the community, and the world.
4. Understand that conflict is an everyday part of life that provides opportunities for growing and learning.
5. Solve problems without whining, complaining, tattling, and blaming others.
6. Develop positive ways to respond to conflict without hitting or fighting.

7. Lose their fear of conflict.
8. Solve problems instead of seeking revenge or getting even.

THE CLIMATE OF RESPECT

When parents gain emotional maturity, they're able to model good conflict resolution skills for their children. Example is a powerful way of teaching our kids how to get along with each other. Kids tend to handle conflict the way they see us handle it. In fact, the handling of conflict can be passed down from generation to generation. An entire family can get a reputation for fighting and feuding. Therefore, the first step in teaching conflict resolution is to keep your cool when everyone else is losing theirs. Once again we're reminded that the caring and supportive environment is our responsibility.

What should you do when two of your children have engaged in a big fight? Well, you should walk toward the conflict slowly. If you're lucky, it'll be over before you get there. However, if you see blood or hair, get there quick. When you arrive on the scene, stand for a moment without saying a word. The silence will help you gather your thoughts and remind you, "I can take care of this situation." Silence is one of your most powerful techniques—use it. As you model calm and patience, your children will be more likely to be calm and patient.

When a fight between two of your children doesn't end when you enter the combat zone, what should you do next? First of all, separate your two fighters. Then ask them to sit together. If necessary, you can sit between them until they calm down and cool off. You can say, "That's enough. Both of you go to your corners." The important step here is to separate the children and allowing for a time-out or "between rounds" period.

Now you can listen to both sides of the story and allow each child to express his or her feelings about the cause of the fight. Then you can ask them to consider other ways to resolve the conflict. "Fighting fair" means allowing each person to say why they are so mad without interruption and coming up with an agreement both children can accept. With your patience and teaching, your children will learn to resolve conflicts without resorting to hitting each other. The other goal is to get your children to resolve fights without involving you. At first, you may need to take a more active role in brainstorming solutions, but try to ease yourself out of the process as soon as possible. As parenting expert Thomas Gordon, author of the wonderful *Parent Effectiveness Training,* says, your children need to "own" the problem to motivate them to resolve it.

One mom I know encouraged her kids to work it out without her by saying, "I know two solutions to this problem. There's my solution, which is boring because I'll either separate you or take away the toy you're fighting about. And then there's your solution, which you'll both like because you came up with it. Go for it."

Increasingly, the response of children to conflict is fighting. Much of the reason for this can be traced to the way our culture portrays violence. For example, if we were taught to see conflict as a contest, we will probably stand our ground and fight physically with our opponent until one of us has won and the other has been soundly defeated. The whole idea of fighting is deeply ingrained in our basic understanding of life. Parents tell me, "I teach my kids to stand up for themselves." "If somebody hits you, you better hit them back." To engage in teaching alternatives to fighting, you must realize that you're swimming upstream against powerful cultural forces.

Fighting is in Our Language

Conflict resolution through fighting has a long history. It's embedded in our language. For example, take a look at the following metaphorical construct:

Argument is war. We conceive of and structure arguments as military campaigns. A vivid example of how deep this metaphor is in our culture can be seen in the popular corporate text, *The Art of War* by Sun Tzu. I challenge you to use language about argument that's not taken from military and war vocabulary. It's virtually impossible to talk about argument in our country without using the language of war. Children grow up in this linguistic atmosphere, so we shouldn't be surprised when they fight with each other. In fact, with or without our permission our children imbibe the warrior mentality.

"Argument is war" is reflected in the way we talk to each other about arguing.

- Your claims are *indefensible.*
- He *attacked every weak point* in my argument.
- His criticisms were *right on target.*
- I *demolished* his argument.
- I've never *won* an argument with him.
- You disagree? Okay, *shoot!*
- If you use that *strategy,* he'll *wipe you out.*
- He *shot down* all my arguments.

We're determined to win or lose arguments. We actually consider the person we're arguing with as the enemy or opponent. We attack and we defend. We gain and lose ground. We plan and plot and use strategies. Our battles may start out verbal and end up in physical conflict. Our children are trained in the fine art of combat simply by listening to us.

Parents often encourage aggressive behavior with their verbal messages:

- "You better not back down when somebody tries to push you around."
- "People are out to get you. They'll screw you if you don't watch your back."
- "If somebody hits you, I expect you to hit them back."
- "Don't be a wimp. Stand up for yourself."
- "Don't ever be a coward. Only cowards run away."

Fighting Is in Our Popular Culture

Children are exposed to and involved in acts of violence from television, movies, and video games. Although it is difficult to establish the casual connection between media violence and violence in children, it seems clear that our culture often gives kids the message that the way to solve problems is to use physical or verbal violence. Visually and linguistically, a mind-set of aggressiveness is established in children.

Children imitate the aggressiveness of their parents and the violence of media characters. They watch movies and television shows that consistently portray violence as the answer to eliminating the "bad guys." Boys are often encouraged to assume roles of physical superiority and dominance. In these repeated media scenarios, the only approved techniques for dealing with one's feelings involve evasiveness, bravado, boasting, bluster, lying, arguing, threatening, and various forms of aggression. With words, visual pictures, and media representations, our popular culture passes on a "kick-butt" competitiveness to our children.

Children need our help in sorting through the powerful messages about aggression, fighting, and power. Parents can help children form alternative understandings about conflict. After all, conflict is a natural part of life. Fighting is only one way to respond to conflict. Children can be taught to come up with a better way of resolving their own conflicts.

How to Get Your Kids to Stop Fighting

Try to imagine a culture where arguments are not treated as battles. There are no winners and no losers. Instead of a fight, an argument is seen as a dance. The children are not seen as opponents but as performers. The goal is to perform in a beautiful and pleasing way. Don't be surprised if you have trouble imagining such a culture. Perhaps the most neutral way of describing this difference between that imaginary culture and ours would be to say that we see arguments in terms of battle and they see arguments structured in terms of dance. What I propose is that we teach more dancing and less fighting. We can help our children structure their understanding of conflict in less violent ways. In other words, the goal becomes working together to understand each other and resolve conflict without fighting.

What can parents do to minimize sibling rivalry? We can teach a set of attitudes, skills, and behaviors that reduce conflict in the family and resolves the normal conflicts that do crop up in positive and productive ways. Many conflicts happen due to false assumptions, refusal to accept responsibility, manipulation and threats, temper tantrums, personal attacks, and refusals to communicate.

I suggest the following initial steps to reduce the intensity of sibling rivalry:

1. Create the expectation that your children will get along. Make sure the rule is clear: "No hitting."
2. Model good conflict resolution skills for your children.

3. Make sure your children understand that you will not tolerate fighting.
4. When children fight, make sure there are real consequences for the misbehavior.
5. Encourage children to solve their own problems.

Research has shown that even very young children are strongly hurt by conflict between their parents. However, they need to learn that disagreement is a routine part of life. It is your responsibility to model how to handle conflict when it arises. Here are some guidelines you should follow:

1. Don't scream, curse, and hit.
2. Don't criticize your spouse in front of your child.
3. Don't give your spouse the "silent treatment."
4. Don't ask your child to choose sides.
5. Don't begin a disagreement in front of your child unless you plan to finish it. Kids need to see that adults can disagree and arrive at a fair compromise.
6. Express your feelings with words as much as possible.
7. Model anger control. If you're going to lose it, say, "I need to calm down. I'll be back in a few minutes." Keep your word.
8. Resolve conflicts and make up in front of your child.
9. If you criticize, use specific language. "I felt disappointed that you didn't keep your promise to pick up the dry cleaning," not "You always break your promises."

One of the most important concepts you can teach your kids is to fight fair. That means disagreeing respectfully, without bullying, histrionics, or dishonesty. Here are some guidelines:

1. Be honest when you're upset or angry. Say so in an upset or angry tone of voice without screaming or shouting.

2. Tell the other person how you feel and why you feel that way. "I feel angry because you were rude to me."

3. State your belief out loud but avoid "killer statements." A killer statement is a personal attack on another person's character. For example, "You can't do anything right." "You aren't very bright." "Is that the best you can do?"

4. Close the time gap between the hurt and the expression of that hurt. Don't stew for an hour, day, or week. Addressing the issue quickly emphasizes cause and effect.

5. Give direct feedback. "I would appreciate it if you would not call me names."

6. State what you want from the other person. "I would like you to accept my feelings."

7. Be open to the other person's point of view on the situation. Point of view is a difficult skill for children to learn, but it's essential. Redford and Virginia Williams, authors of *Lifeskills,* say, "You're only listening if you're prepared to be changed by what you hear."

8. Negotiate an agreement that you both can accept.

9. Call time-out if you find yourself losing control of your temper.

10. Refuse to take abuse. "It isn't acceptable for you to speak to me that way. We don't allow name-calling in this house."

11. Insist on fair treatment.

DEALING WITH FEELINGS

You want to help your children know that feelings are okay. Often children struggle with mixed messages about feelings. When I was growing up in the hills of northern Louisiana, we were often told by the men in our small community that "big boys don't cry; big boys can hold their liquor; big boys take care of the girls." I refer to these teachings as a Ph.D. in redneck philosophy. What do you get when a boy is raised according to these tenets of hegemonic masculinity? well, you get a heavy-drinking male sexist with no feelings. They're not in high demand in the new century.

Feelings are real. Feelings are legitimate. Have you ever tried to stop a feeling? It's all right to be happy, concerned, joyful, sad, angry, frustrated, and hurt. Parents often make the mistake of attacking the feelings of their children rather than their behavior. Feelings are indicators that something is not right or something needs changing. Feelings, then, are amoral. They're not good, they're not bad, they just are. "Don't tell me how to feel" is a good response to someone who's attacking your feelings. It's what we do with our feelings of anger or hurt that we're responsible for. I can be angry and let that anger consume me as I strike out in rage at anyone and anything around me, or I can recognize that feeling as a warning sign that I need to change. The choice is mine. Choice, then, is the key concept to communicate to your children.

One way to help children understand feelings is to talk about your own feelings. If your fourth-grader comes home angry over something that happened at school, you can identify with that anger. Acknowledge that he's upset, don't belittle his feelings. ("You got all wound up over a recess game?") Tell him about a time when you were angry at school. Tell him how you felt and what you did to feel better. Another good way to teach that feelings are okay is to list things that make you angry. Go over them with your child. Explain what happened the last time you got angry. Tell your child how to handle your anger.

If we don't take the time to explore feelings and attitudes with our children, we increase the chance of passing along negative feelings and responses to them.

Lucy Marsden, the main character in Allan Gurganus's *Oldest Living Confederate Widow Tells All,* says:

> My mother once me that, that, of all electric feelings on life's totem pole of bargain-basement emotions, Jealousy and Self-Pity are the tackiest. Momma always felt more at ease lecturing about emotion than showing any. Still, this didn't make her wrong concerning personal hunches. I remember her changing subjects, claiming every local family had its own built-in gene-prone weaknesses. Ketchums stole. Cogdells stuttered. The Williamses always suffered kidney complaints and, after forty years, their backs went. So I asked, "What's ours?" She blinked. I pressed her, being pushy me, "What's our own clan's biggest sicknesses?" Momma got a strange large look on her narrow face. She felt to check if her cameo was pinned on strait. She looked dead ahead as her voice wobbled some. "Jealousy and Self-Pity," she said.

Dealing with children's negative feelings is a tough job for parents. The tendencies are to ignore the child, deny the child's feelings, or moralize and filibuster.

Children are not that competent at expressing their feelings. The journey from the heart to the lips is a difficult one for children. Children are not that good at analyzing their feelings. After all, I know grown people who can't verbalize the nature of their feelings.

Often children simply don't know why they feel as they do. Other times, they're afraid of expressing their true feelings. Parents who badger children with constant questions end up sounding like prosecuting attorneys.

Acknowledgment is more important than agreement. Children don't always need our advice. They always need understanding and compassion and empathy.

Parents need to be specific rather than general. Instead of saying, "I understand how you feel," be specific and concrete. "You're mad because you didn't get to sit next to your friend." "You feel sad because Ashley didn't invite you to the party."

When children are angry, they say words that can hurt. As a parent, you need the emotional maturity not to take such verbal attacks personally. You can, however, gently correct your child: "In our house, we don't say such things." I tend to ignore expressions of frustration by my children as long as they're not attacking my character.

Accepting your children's feelings doesn't mean you're being a pushover. It isn't the same as allowing child to act inappropriately. When children know we understand them, they'll be more understanding of the limits imposed on them.

Here are some guidelines for dealing with feelings.

1. Acknowledge your own feelings and name them.
2. Admit that you're angry, hurt, or afraid.
3. Do something responsible and purposeful to address your feelings.
4. Make assertive statements about yourself.
5. Acknowledge your children's feelings.
6. Don't be judgmental or critical or defensive.
7. Teach your children to handle their own feelings assertively.

ACTIVITIES AND GAMES FOR HELPING CHILDREN UNDERSTAND FEELINGS

Since children are such visual learners, I believe that parents should incorporate hands-on activities like those used in elementary classrooms to teach their children basic conflict skills.

Egg-citing emotions You will need one egg carton and twelve plastic eggs that open. Inside each egg put a small piece of paper with an emotion written on it. Ask your child to pick an egg, pull out the piece of paper on the inside, and silently read the emotion written there. He or she will then act out the emotion and you will try to guess what is being dramatized. This can be a fun game to play with younger children, who might need a third player to read, then whisper the emotion to them. You can also take turns drawing an egg out of the carton and acting out the enclosed emotion.

Create a feeling chart. You will need a large sheet of chart paper and a number of 6-by-10-inch cards with the following words written on them: *happy, excited, lonely, proud, mad, jealous, scared, surprised, sad, angry,* and *worried.* Display each word and discuss its meaning with your children. Talk about times when the children have felt the feeling written on the card. Put the index cards on the chart paper. Have your children pantomime how each feeling looks.

How do you feel? Make a list of sentences that involve various feelings. Read each sentence to your child and ask him or her to fill in the blank with the feeling that best describes how he or she feels at the moment.

- When someone pushes me, I feel _____.
- When I make a mistake, I feel _____.
- When I do a good job, I feel _____.
- When I help someone and they say "Thanks," I feel ____.

- When someone calls me a name, I feel _____.
- When someone won't share with me, I feel _____.
- When someone smiles at me, I feel _____.
- When someone tries to push me around, I feel _____.

The Anger Thermometer. You will need an actual thermometer and a drawing of an anger thermometer. The purpose of this visual lesson is to demonstrate to your children that different experiences call for different degrees of response. By using this visual aid, you will be able to help your children understand that there are various degrees of anger.

We don't make the same response to everything that happens to us. For example, your six-year-old can learn that every little thing that happens doesn't call for an enraged temper tantrum. Show a thermometer to your children and ask them to describe what a thermometer does. Explain that a higher, hotter temperature means the red mercury rises. Show them the anger thermometer that you have drawn and explain that when people get angry, it's as if they get hotter. The angrier they are, the more fever they have. For example, "Hot under the collar," is an old expression for anger, as is "He really blew his top." Anger can be measure on the anger thermometer. The more intense the emotions, the higher the red line rises. The anger thermometer will have the following terms listed on it, from the least to most intense: Annoyed, Irritated, Angry, Furious, and Enraged. Now give your child a few examples of behavior that makes them mad and ask them to point to the response on the anger thermometer that parallels their response.

Here are some sample scenarios to try with your child:

- Your brother takes the video game away from you and screams, "Mine, mine."

- Your sister says, "You can't sit here. I own this seat."
- You want to swing, but your brothers who are on the swings won't get off.
- Your big sister won't let you sit by the window in the car.

You will also want to discuss the results of the activity with your children. What things made you the angriest? What things didn't bother you very much? Did you feel the same way about every situation? What can you do to cool off if you're hot on the anger thermometer? (Take a deep breath, count to 10, smile, walk away.)

Why should parents take the time to teach children conflict resolution skills? Children are not natural resolvers of conflict; they just do what comes naturally. Socialization is a learned skill. Conflict is normal, routine, and natural. Conflict happens. Your kids didn't invent sibling rivalry. Kids need a framework, a way of dealing with the inevitable disagreements. Learning conflict resolution builds resiliency. It also gives kids social competence, problem-solving ability, autonomy, a sense of purpose and hope.

Build bridges instead of blowing them up and having to rebuild them every day. What's the payoff? Is it worth the time and trouble? You're going to deal with conflict on a regular basis. You might as well teach while dealing with it.

For the parents there are a number of worthy benefits. As with establishing routines, home life will be more pleasant. There will be more peace and quiet with less noise in the house. Stress will be reduced. Children will gain cooperative skills and generate goodwill in the family. Problems will have true solutions with longer-lasting results.

The children will also benefit in the following ways:

- Improved self-discipline
- Better relationships with siblings

- Better attitudes (no chip on the shoulder)
- Improved interpersonal relationship skills
- Stronger, more supportive home environment

DIRECTING CONFLICT TRAFFIC
IN THE FAMILY

On some days my home has looked like a bumper car ride at a carnival and all my drivers have road rage. Other days were like rush-hour traffic jams. I felt there was a need for some traffic signals to direct conflicts and problems among my children. I would hold up my hand as the traffic cop and say "Red," "Yellow," or "Green." Teach your kids these emotional traffic signals:

RED: Stop and think.
        Cool down.
        Don't jump to conclusions.
        Don't blame, criticize, or judge others.

YELLOW: Be cautious.
        Go slow.
        Take inventory of assumptions, feelings and
           thoughts.
        Look in all directions and try to understand the
           point of view of others.
        Pay attention to how others feel.
        Hold back, stand still, and be quiet.
        Acknowledge their feelings.
        Resist giving advice, opinion, or philosophy.

GREEN: Come up with a plan.
        Go for the goal.
        Pick a road and go for it!
        How did things turn out?

You can set the stage for teaching your kids about conflict resolution by instilling in them some core skills:

1. Teach the basic skills of optimism: "I can solve this problem." "If I do this differently, it'll turn out better next time." "If I work at it, I can make this come out." Optimistic kids believe in their own abilities to solve problems; their optimistic outlook is infectious to others. Encourage your child to take an optimistic point of view.

2. Ensure that your children feel competent in something. Kids often get angry if they perceive that they "fail at everything." Help your child achieve mastery in something and remind him of that ability: "You worked hard to achieve that; you can do it again." Helping your child become competent teaches him that efforts produce results; if you work at problems, you can solve them.

3. Give your children opportunities to "influence" others. If your child is angry at a younger sibling for swiping his toy, you can help turn that anger into pride and empathy by asking him, to "show Johnny how to share." Encourage your kids to "show Rachel how you would handle that problem" or "help Juan figure out how to cool down."

4. Practice problem-solving strategies in real-life situations. "Kids, we have to be at the recital in half an hour and no one's taken any showers or gotten ready. What should we do next?" "You promised your sister you would baby-sit on Friday and now you want to go to the movies with your friends instead. How can you work this out?" "Going to soccer camp for a week costs $100. What's your plan for coming up with some money?"

5. Encourage classroom teachers to provide support to children for ordinary problems. Ask them if they can make conflict resolution part of their curriculum.

6. Use the language of high expectancy: "I expect you to control your temper." "I know you know how to use your words." "I won't solve this problem for you—you and your brother need to find a way to work it out so you're both happy, and I expect you not to give up until you find a solution."

7. Model empathy, caring, and helpfulness: "I can see how angry you two are. Why don't you see how you can resolve this?" If your kids push you to take sides or resolve the fight, calmly but politely refuse. "I know you two will find a fair solution." Help only if they are truly stuck by offering leading questions, not piling on advice.

8. Walk the talk. If you can't resolve your own problems without yelling, losing your temper, caving in, or stewing, you need to improve your own conflict resolution skills before you can reasonably expect your kids to have them. Take a course or seek out a therapist who can help.

9. Teach social skills in ways that promote learning the skill. If you're trying to teach your kids that they must always be polite and respectful, even when disagreeing, model that behavior—even, especially—when you're upset yourself.

10. Ask your kids how they would do something differently if what they did produced a negative outcome. "What could you do next time so this wouldn't happen again?" If your child shrugs or says, "I dunno," keep pressing gently for solutions, don't immediately leap in with them yourself.

A child who has mastered good conflict resolution skills is more:

- Open-minded
- Tolerant of diverse opinions
- Empathetic
- Accepting of differing point of view
- Patient
- Balanced
- Friendly
- Far-sighted
- Inclined to seek solutions
- Altruistic

SOLVING CONFLICTS

Children need to learn a variety of ways to solve conflicts. There are various strategies for de-escalating and resolving conflict.

- *Talk it out.* Sitting down and talking can solve many conflicts. "I know you are really upset with me because I wouldn't let you go out this weekend. Let's talk about the problem. Tell me your side first."
- *Listen to each other.* People in conflict need to be willing to listen to each other. Good listening helps each person understand what the other is thinking and feeling.
- *Share.* If people are having a conflict about who gets to use something, there may be a way to share. "I know that both of you want to watch a different television program right now. I need you to come up with a way that you can both get something you want. So sit down and make a deal to cover the next few nights."

- *Take turns.* One way to share is to decide that first one person uses it, and then the other person has a turn. "Remember, we take turns on the swing." If your children are having trouble sharing the swing or a toy, you can set a timer to ring every five minutes. Each time the timer rings, another child has his or her turn. With daily practice, taking turns will become a routine.

- *Compromise.* If both people give in a little, they may solve the problem. If two of your children are fighting over a toy, your can take the toy away from both of them. Then ask them to come up with a way that each child can have some time to use that particular toy. "I will keep the toy until the two of you arrive at a plan for sharing."

- *Make a peace offering.* One person gives a little gift or something that shows he or she wants to resolve the misunderstanding.

- *Say, "I'm sorry."*

- *Build trust.* Sometimes one person doesn't believe what the other person says. People can learn to trust one another by building a library of occasions during which they've demonstrated trust.

- *Work together.* Sometimes agreeing to work together can solve a conflict.

- *Solve the problem.* Conflicts are problems. If the people solve the problem, then the conflict ends.

- *Put it off.* Sometimes people are too angry to talk it out or solve the problem. They may need to take a time-out. They may need a cooling-down period. Teach your kids that taking a break isn't being a quitter or a coward, it's being very grown-up.

- *Skip it.* Some conflicts aren't worth bothering with in terms of time and effort. Just forget about it. Teach your kids to ask themselves, "Is this really worth fighting about?"

- *Get help.* Sometimes you need to ask a grown-up or another child to help you.

EXERCISES TO HELP YOUR CHILD LEARN COOPERATION AND CONSIDERATION

Trace your hand. Have your son or daughter trace one hand on a piece of paper. Then ask him or her to write a friend's name or a sibling's name in the palm of the hand. Ask your son or daughter to write five positive facts about that person with one sentence on each finger.

Mirror, Mirror. Two of your children are paired with each other to work cooperatively. One sibling holds a mirror in front of his or her face while the other one asks: "Mirror, mirror, say what you see. Tell what you like best about me."

From the beginning of your parenting life, teach your children that there are viable alternatives to conflict. When given the proper tools, kids can and do come up with a productive plan to solve their own conflicts. For example, consider the following constructive alternative.

1. Come up with a plan. Instead of solving all problems for your children, teach them how to devise their own solutions. Don't rush in with advice or proscriptions. Encourage your kids to make a plan that will work for both of them. You can help them along when they're stuck, but they're more likely to buy into a solution they've thought of themselves.
2. Look at all the different points of view. Your children will

often be confused by the fact that everyone doesn't see things exactly the same way. An important step in teaching kids to get along is helping them accept the perspective of their siblings.

3. Be honest and express your real feelings.
4. Use common sense.
5. Agree on the action that each child will take to carry out the plan.

When two of your children are fighting over a toy, you will probably hear them say, "It's mine." "I want it." "Give it to me." "I'm going to take it away from you." Instead of having an emotional outburst, guide your children through the five steps to resolving conflict. First, walk over to your children, hold out your hand, and say, "Give me the toy." Then ask the children to sit down to talk. You can help them understand how each one of them feels about the situation. ("Anil, you feel mad because you had the toy first. Padma, you're upset because you think Anil was having too long a turn.") Your children may not have a revelation about seeing each other's point of view today, but with time, patience, and practice, they will learn. Spend some time helping your children express their feelings about the toy and about not wanting the other one to have the toy. Most of all, make sure that the children devise their own plan for sharing the toy.

There will also be times when your best efforts at teaching conflict resolution fail. A child may become more and more aggressive. At this point, instead of loading the child with more and more punishment, you need to consider other alternatives. Discipline plans are no longer helpful at this point. You may need to accept the reality that you are no longer able to be objective or to offer help. The aggression and misbehavior can't be allowed to continue so you should seek professional care for your child. This isn't a failure, it's a wise, responsible choice.

HELPING YOUR CHILD SEE THE OTHER POINT OF VIEW

Understanding other points of view is an essential skill in getting along and resolving conflict. When kids have arguments, there are numerous sides to what happened. This difference in perspective is the very heart of conflict. Developmentally, children have a hard time seeing any other point of view than their own. Children can, however, learn to look at different points of views in a conflict.

You can read one of the following books to your children: *The True Story of the Three Little Pigs* by Jon Scieszka, *The Pain and the Great One* by Judy Blume, or *The Knight and the Dragon* by Tomie dePaola.

In teacher workshops, I often ask small groups to rewrite the story of Cinderella from the point of view of the stepmother. The entire story changes when seen through her eyes. You can help your children understand that people have different ways of looking at things. Since we have different bodies, different families, and different experiences, we see the world differently.

Perception is based on past experiences. Our experience, values, attitudes, traditions, prejudices, cultural assumptions, religious background, and family of origin are all part of our perception. The way we were raised by our parents impacts how we raise our own children. Who took charge in your home? How did things get done? Who did all the housework? Each person has his or her own point of view or perspective. Understanding another point of view is crucial to our ability to listen with empathy to our children.

We have to help our children defuse the idea that the family is a hierarchical social order in which they're either one-up or one-down. Our children need to have the security that they live in a positive home environment of closeness, confirmation, support, and consensus. Life isn't a war but a community. As parents, we must strive to create a community of intimacy and connection.

CHAPTER 9

ENCOURAGING DISCIPLINE

DISCIPLINE IS A TEACHING PRACTICE. The word *discipline* comes from the word *disciple,* and a disciple is a student or a learner. When parents discipline children properly, they're teaching them responsibility and self-control. As indicated in earlier chapters, the key to discipline isn't making your children behave, but making sure that as a parent you exercise self-discipline and self-control. Discipline is an attitude. When parents are able to convey the message "I'm in charge," they're better able to exercise real discipline. Being in charge, however, doesn't include being rude, loud, obnoxious, or out of control.

Encouraging discipline is a method for teaching children to be responsible for their own behavior. As you demonstrate good behavior, your children are more likely to catch by osmosis the way they're expected to behave. For example, here are some basic discipline guidelines we use in my home:

1. The rules in our family must be fair.
2. We must clearly define our family rules and explain them to our children.
3. Our rules apply only to behavior that has a direct effect on the family or home, not to matters that are trivial. Among these trivial matters are children having arguments that go

around and around without becoming aggressive. You can ignore these conversations and stay out of the way. The clothes your children wear, the pierced ears on your teenage son, the way your daughter wears her hair, spilled milk at the breakfast table, and minor disagreements are trivial matters that don't require discipline. Children are allowed the privilege of being children. We should avoid the trap of "microparenting." Hovering over children like helicopters can be an exhausting task. Microparenting produces a lot of negative, proscriptive communication: "Stop that." "Put that down." "Don't put that in your mouth." "What in the world are you doing?" "How many times do I have to tell you to shut up?" "Give me that." "Get out of there." If we want to create a positive home environment, we can't come down on our kids for every little thing. Does that hairstyle or outfit have a direct effect on the family or home?

4. Our children should understand the rules and the consequences of breaking them. Rules and consequences are established in advance. This means that we're not going to wait until we get irritated or out of control and dish out extreme consequences to our children. For example, that means no spanking, ever.

5. Rules don't change without discussions with our children. We practice democracy in our home. I realize there is a paradox within the concept of the parents "being in charge" and having democracy in the home. What I try to accomplish is a balance between these polarities in my family's life.

For example, we have a family meeting to discuss behavior and rules. Everyone has a chance to speak. Each of my children has status as a valuable member of the family. All of them have equal voice. That is the democratic side of our family. When ultimate decisions have to be made, Johnelle and I are in charge. However, we treat our children with respect. Being in charge doesn't mean rude, crude, obnoxious, manipulative, or punitive behavior on our part. I'm not trying to prove how tough I am; I am working to teach my children to be independent human beings. In that sense we practice democracy.

One of my favorite books is *King Louie Katz,* by Dr. Seuss. King Louie, the king of Katzen-stein, has another cat to hold his royal tail and keep it from dragging on the ground. To get to the end of a long story (no puns intended), every cat has another cat to hold up his tail. But the last cat in the line hasn't a soul to hold up his tail. And so he cries, "I quit." He slams the tail of the cat in front of him to the ground. The end result: "And since that day in Katzen-stein, all cats have been more grown up. They're all more demo-catic because each cat holds his own up." That's the spirit of independence that I strive to teach, and democracy is a big part of that teaching.

6. We involve our children in making home rules. We discuss rules and why we need them. When certain behaviors of our children become routine, there is no longer any need for a rule in that area. For example, when each of our children puts away toys at the end of the day, we don't need a rule that says, "Clean your room and pick up all your toys." Our children are allowed to question rules as well as consequences. We work hard to reach consensus whenever possible. After getting input from all the members of our family, Johnelle and I make the final decisions about rules.

The children usually come up with fifteen to twenty rules, and we choose the four most important rules. Again, rules aren't necessary for minor infractions such as little arguments children have, mistakes they make while moving fast (e.g., stepping on the dog's tail, forgetting to shut the door, walking in puddles, playing in the dirt, getting hyperactive during long sermons at church, knocking over a vase, or getting really loud), playing their music loud, wearing weird clothes, using teenage slang, not eating everything on the plate, or not going to sleep exactly on time. Rigid and excessive rules can create a stressful and angry home climate.

7. There is fair and firm enforcement of family rules. There aren't bigger consequences if Dad is ticked off, or no consequences if Mom can't be bothered. We are consistent.

8. Children take responsibility for their actions. Our job as parents center on teaching responsibility. In my parenting workshops, I often ask, "What do you most want your children to learn before they are grown?" The answer I hear most often is, "I want my children to be responsible."

9. My wife and I mutually support each other's decisions. One of the biggest areas of difficulty for parents has nothing to do with the misbehavior of children. It has to do with parents not being on the same page. One parent believes in a particular discipline and the other parent disagrees. The most-asked questions at my parenting workshops deal with Mom and Dad disagreeing over discipline methods. There is a lot of stress and pain when parents don't support each other's decisions. There have been times when Johnelle has been frustrated by my tendency to be too permissive. The resulting tension has impacted our

marriage in negative ways. With time and understanding, we have learned to resolve this issue.

One day Johnelle said, "The next time our children get you cornered, I want you to break free. Come find me, and I will stand by you, hold you, help you to be strong, and together we will deal with our children." That taught me one of the most practical parenting lessons I have ever learned. The best parenting work is done together. Of course this doesn't apply to single parents, but if you're raising children together, stand together when you discipline the children. They recognize your unified front, and they realize there isn't a court of appeal. I recommend that parents get on the same page before they ever begin any discipline of their children.

10. Rules that are made are enforced. Consistency is the most important principle.

11. Parents are in charge and in control.

12. When children break the rules, they all receive the same treatments.

13. Consequences for breaking rules are appropriate and don't take away from children's dignity. One of the major concerns of parents attending my workshops is the idea of appropriate consequences. A consequence is a nonpunitive discipline that gets your child's attentions. For example, not being allowed to play outside can be a consequence for your child not doing his or her homework. Consequences are as fair as possible and they don't show disrespect for the child. Punishment, on the other hand, is an arbitrary action by an adult that demeans, degrades, and hurts a child. The most obvious form of punishment is spanking. Children have the opportunity to avoid consequences by

making good choices. In my view, a child receives consequences in order to teach a particular lesson. Punishment isn't teaching.

14. Minor misbehavior doesn't get more attention than it deserves. Once again, the idea is to avoid "microparenting" practices. The tension, the stress, and the anxiety produced by monitoring every little detail of a child's life aren't worth the effort.

15. We don't let small problems grow into larger ones. When there is a problem, we deal with it immediately. We don't allow problems to hang around our home unresolved. We make a consistent attempt to solve problems and move on. Allowing problems to fester and grow can infect the family atmosphere and create all kinds of negative results.

16. We will address behavior problems immediately. Emotional "leftovers" create additional problems. Besides, people quickly tire of leftovers. I'm amazed that after every Thanksgiving, I have a craving for pizza by Saturday evening. I'm so tired of turkey sandwiches I could scream. Deal with problems and issues of misbehavior as quickly as possible.

17. We're comfortable disciplining our children. "I love you, therefore I discipline you." Parents have to rid themselves of the false idea that discipline is the opposite of love. To not discipline a child is to spoil a child, and that's unacceptable.

18. We have high expectations and goals for our children.

19. We allow our children to make as many choices as possible.

20. We have established routines for our children.

21. We check our own attitude. Check yours every morning

before you face the children. The emotional cup of vitamin C is essential for a good day when dealing with children.

22. We use strategies designed to prevent behavior problems.

23. We discipline our child's behavior not his or her character. We say, "I'm disappointed because you did _____"; not "I'm disappointed because you are _____."

24. We handle discipline in private as often as possible. This shows respect for the feelings of our children.

PROBLEMS PARENTS ENCOUNTER

Parents show up at my workshops with particular discipline problems in mind. Most of their attention is focused on what's wrong with their child. I have noticed an amazing rationalization on the part of many parents when it comes to their own ineffective behavior. Parents will openly tell me that they lose their temper, yell and scream, threaten, and spank their children. They also indicate a preference for telling children over and over to go to bed or pick up their toys or eat their broccoli. A typical response goes like this: "I know I shouldn't scream at my kids, but I'm so tired and I lose it so easily." There is little connection between the emotional state of the parent and the resultant emotional outburst from the child.

Recently a parent asked me how to get her two-year-old son to stop taking a bottle at night. She said that nothing was working. The little boy would get up "fifty times" a night if she didn't give him his bottle at bedtime. Mom was totally frustrated and at the end of her rope. I told her to give her son his bottle and let him go to sleep. There isn't any reason to create unnecessary conflict. I also suggested that she make sure she fed him a good solid meal for dinner. If she felt that it was time to wean her son from the bottle, I suggested she fill it with water. At some point, she needed to decide to deal with the issue and put him back to bed without a bottle as many times as necessary until he learned to stay in bed without it.

Other parents struggle with sibling rivalry. Children won't do their homework. Children won't stay put in time-out.

Adults become too easily frustrated by their kids' immature behavior. Remember, the keys are consistency and cumulative effects. Hang in there and keep at the discipline. Children will come around to your point of view with time and patience.

Many of the problems caused between parents and children can be traced to the inability of grown people to maintain self-control. Much of the material in this book has been designed to teach you self-control. Your children catch your attitude as surely as they catch a virus that's passed around the whole family. The morning attitude check before facing the children is a necessity. Please don't let your own bad attitude deprive your children of a better future.

At my workshops I'm often amazed at the kinds of simple problems that confound, confuse, and infuriate parents. There is a sense of panic and paranoia about the most insignificant concerns. I hear so many parents fuss about their children's diet, but often pay no attention to their mental and emotional consumption from watching excessive amounts of television. Other parents monitor children's books and carry on the censorship campaigns. Some parents are trying to get Harry Potter books out of school libraries because some overzealous ancestor of Salem has decided the books teach witchcraft and the occult. My observation is that Harry Potter has children excited about reading, and that can only be a good thing.

Parents have to learn from experience not to sweat the small stuff. That means figuring out by trial and error what is and what isn't big stuff. Please hold your child accountable for his own behavior. If a child figures out that you're making excuses for bad behavior at school, he will act out more and more. Showing up at school with your lawyer to attack a minor discipline problem sends a bad message to children. Minor misbehavior shouldn't get more attention than it deserves.

I'm also amazed at how simplistic people can be in their usual approaches to parenting. I see one extreme or the other: permissive or hard-nosed. Critical thinking is replaced by tradition. Older adults piously intone that children are out of control because mothers are at work in the office instead of at home with the children. Time isn't the issue. Working moms isn't the issue. Relationships, communication, and solid parenting skills are more important.

DISCIPLINE STRATEGIES FOR PARENTS

Discipline means getting your child's attention and helping him or her learn to take responsibility for inappropriate behavior without being mean, crude, rude, or loud. The important fact to keep in mind is that when a discipline strategy doesn't work, you should try a new strategy. You should announce your intentions so that your children get the message: "What I have been trying hasn't worked with you. Therefore, today we're beginning a new system of discipline. Keep in mind that I'm never going to give up and that you're expected to behave yourself and follow the rules."

Creative Discipline

With the strategy called creative discipline, parents observe, listen to, and evaluate what is really important to their children and tie their consequences to those important things. If your child adores Nintendo, you might make losing Nintendo privileges for a set time a consequence of misbehavior. Taking away a beloved game or toy may appear harsh, but the child needs to learn that bad behavior produces serious consequences. Hundreds of parents have complained to me that they've tried taking away privileges from their children and the results have been disappointing. Part of the problem lies in parents giving up too soon. Another part of the problem arises from parents not knowing which privileges really matter to their children. An even larger problem is parents not having the courage to actually take away important privileges from their children.

For example, I was having a difficult time convincing Jeffrey that good grades were important. The first six weeks of school when he was in the eleventh grade, Jeffrey made three C's on his report card. Needless to say, I was not a happy daddy. My normally straight-A son was dragging through school on cruise control. I was angry and I told him so in no uncertain terms. I also said, "Jeffrey, these C's have to go. You should be making all A's. What do you intend to do about this?" "I'll try to study harder," he responded. That was only an excuse to get out of a serious conversation with me.

I considered a number of alternatives. First, I thought about grounding him for the upcoming six weeks. But I have never had much success with grounding children for long periods of time. In fact, the person getting punished in grounding situations is usually the parent. Why should we punish ourselves? We didn't do anything wrong. So I decided not to ground Jeffrey.

Then I thought about yelling at him and threatening him. Nothing good would come out of me venting my frustration in such ineffective ways. So I took a few deep breaths, told myself, "I can handle this," and tried to think of a more creative way to discipline my son. Then I recalled overhearing Jeffrey bragging to two of his friends, "I'm not riding the cheese." Jeffrey calls the school bus "the cheese"—that yellow square on wheels. "I'm not riding the cheese" sounded like music to my ears.

My discipline decisions were now clear. I said, "Jeffrey, you can keep the Jeep and drive it to school every day. I will give you six weeks to bring up those bad grades. At the end of the six weeks, here's our deal: *'If you make C's, you ride the cheese.'"* Jeffrey was shocked, but I could tell that I had his attention. In order to reinforce my discipline, I had him call the transportation director for the school system and find out what bus he would be riding if his grades didn't improve. "Cheese number 267" became my refrain for the next few weeks. At breakfast, I would look across the table at Jeffrey and say, "Cheese." When Jeffrey brought home his next report card, he'd made four A's, three B's, and no C's. I was a happy daddy. As his parent, my job is to help him reach his potential. The fact that he doesn't always like me or my decisions isn't that important. Deep down he knows that I love him.

Creative discipline is for older children ages twelve to eighteen. I use creative discipline for situations that don't lend themselves to more usual discipline techniques. When faced with a specific situation, you can consider coming up with a discipline plan that is more creatively crafted to get your child's attention. The main purpose of creative discipline is to find a calm, somewhat humorous way to achieve a very serious goal.

Creative discipline goes one step further than natural consequences. For example, the natural consequence for going outside on a freezing day without a coat is that your child will get cold. If a child doesn't make it home in time for dinner, the natural consequence would be eating a cold supper alone. Natural consequences are the real-life results of the actions of children. Creative discipline, on the other hand, is a way of giving a child reasonable consequences that help him learn how to act differently next time.

By using your imagination, you can come up with variations of my "C's and cheese" plan. For example, if your child is not coming home at night by midnight according to the rule you have set, but you're not always awake to check on her, you need to find a creative way to address this issue. You can set the alarm clock in your bedroom to go off at midnight. Your child has to come in before midnight, turn off the alarm, and tell you good night. If the alarm goes off and awakens you, obviously your child is still not home and must accept a consequence determined in advance. Being creative keeps you calm and avoids the trap of making up punishments and consequences for every possible violation of a whole host of confusing rules.

Let's review the steps in creative discipline:

1. Consider the various alternatives that are available to you.
2. List the various strategies that you believe will best get your child's attention.
3. Clearly explain your discipline plan to your child.
4. Carry out your discipline plan and make sure you follow through.

THE "GAME" APPROACH TO DISCIPLINE

One of the best ways to discipline children is to construct a strategy built around games. After all, games are designed to be fun. Games are also well organized, with very definite rules. Your children are already accustomed to playing games by the rules. Games take place within predetermined boundaries with a well-defined structure. Games involve strategies. Through games, we can make sure that our discipline is a teaching experience rather than a punitive experience. What I'm suggesting is approaches to discipline that borrow concepts from baseball, soccer, and hockey. We'll transfer what our children know about games to our discipline strategies. While it's not possible to make discipline fun, it's possible to make sure that our discipline treats our children with respect.

I have one other reason for recommending the "game" approach to discipline. More than ever, it's important for fathers to be directly involved in the raising of their children. The old idea that Mom takes care of the children and dishes out all the discipline just won't get the job done. So, I have designed the "game" discipline strategy as a metaphor that Dad will appreciate and understand. This means that Dad will be more likely to learn how to be an effective disciplinarian.

If we think of discipline as a game, we're less likely to have a home environment that's more like a war. It's a lot more effective to play a game than wage a war on the homefront.

THE FOUR STEPS TO DISCIPLINE AS A GAME

Step One: Get a game plan

If you're married, sit down together and make sure that you're in agreement on your goals, your ideas, and your game plan for discipline. In other words, make sure you're both on the same page. Parents disciplining their children together is a powerful and positive method. You're asking for trouble and inconsistency if you fail to have a game plan.

For example, the game plan shouldn't use discipline that ends up punishing you. If you tell your teenager she can't drive the car for a month because she was disrespectful to you at a dinner, this isn't a good game plan. You end up being punished because now you have to drive everyone else to school and take your teenager all the places she has to go for the next thirty days.

If your child allows his room to become a disaster area, you might be tempted to hang a construction zone sign on his door or punish him or give him endless lectures on the importance of a clean room. A better game plan would be to go to your son's room on a Saturday morning and supervise him while he gives his room a complete cleaning that would make a professional maid service proud.

Our game plan called for a consistent application of the basic principles of discipline outlined at the beginning of this chapter. We agreed that we wouldn't spank our children or use any form of punishment that denigrated, degraded, or demeaned our children. We promised that we wouldn't allow our children to be in charge. We were determined to maintain our sense of self-respect and treat our children with the same respect we expected from them.

Step Two: Make the rules for your family

I suggest that you have no more than four or five basic rules at a time. These general rules will be the same for all children. If you have different rules for different children, you will create a mountain of confusion. If you have too many rules, you will be confused and you will probably forget some of your own rules.

Here is a sample list of four rules for our family:

> No screaming, hitting, or fighting.
> Homework will be completed by 8:00 P.M.
> All chores will be finished before going out to play.
> Respect for each other is expected.

Having a few basic rules makes them easier to remember. As a parent you can't work on all areas of your children's behavior at the same time. With a few basic rules, you'll be able to concentrate on the important issues. Remember, you have the right to choose your battles. Your basic rules don't have to cover every possible behavior. After all, you reserve the right to replace one rule with another rule. Rules that you replace remain in force as "unwritten rules."

That way, your children are still responsible for the old rules even though you are no longer focusing on them.

One good way to communicate your rules is to follow the practice of good classroom teachers. Explain your rules carefully and make sure everyone understands them. Make a poster of your rules and hang them on the breakfast room wall or in the hall. Every time your children see the rules, it reinforces them. Then if your children get off to a bad start that morning, you can line them up facing the copy of the rules and have them repeat with you, "I pledge allegiance to our family rules." Every family will have different rules. You may want to concentrate on some general rules that are universal in nature. Sample rules might include showing respect, doing tasks on time, doing what you're asked to do the first time, keeping the house clean, completing homework at a reasonable hour, and completing all chores.

You don't, however, need rules for your family routines. These have already become habits and shouldn't cause trouble once they are ingrained. Once your children become adept at maintaining a particular rule, drop it from the list because it has now become a routine. *If a rule becomes a routine, you no longer need that rule.* Review the rules every few months to make sure they still apply to the situation in your family. Remember, any area of family life that causes chaos needs a rule. Adopting a general rule for trouble spots is the first step toward peace. Parents at my workshops usually list bedtime, chores, mealtime, homework, sibling rivalry, and disrespect as the major battle zones in their homes.

Step Three: Decide on the consequences for not following the rules.

Parents often make rules but neglect to include the consequences. I have discovered through the hard knocks of experience that rules without preattached consequences made me inconsistent and off-the-wall with my discipline. When children violate our rules, we get upset. And upset parents do not always think clearly. You can avoid bad decisions by deciding on the consequences in advance. For example, "If you hit your brother, you will sit in the rocking chair until you can tell us what you will do next time instead of hitting your brother." If your child tells you a lie and then denies it, you should trust your inner feeling. Your child will probably accuse you of not trusting her, but that shouldn't prevent you from giving her consequences for not telling the truth. She should lose her privileges for the rest of the week, and she will have to endure some extra checking up on her claims for a couple of weeks because she can't be trusted to tell the truth. In other words, connect real consequences to the rules. The children will understand what you mean by: "If you violate rule number one, you will spend the entire weekend at home." Once you have established your consequences, you should display them on the poster along with the rules. By connecting rules and consequences you have assured yourself of a measure of consistency that almost guarantees better discipline and better results. There is less confusion and where there is less confusion there is less chaos.

While the general rules should be the same for all your children, consequences should be specific to the age or developmental stage of each child. Your four-year-old will receive different consequences than your teenager. Your children will probably accuse you of being unfair at this point. You may want to remind them, "Life is not always fair." But also point out to your kids that you are being fair with each child in each situation.

Specific Rules for Trouble Areas

Here are some examples of specific rules that you can use for those areas that are trouble spots. Your goal in setting specific rules is to turn rules into routines as quickly as possible.

1. Raise your hand to be excused from the dinner table.
2. Keep the floor in your room clear of toys and all other objects.
3. No cursing.
4. Ask permission to change the television channel.
5. Follow directions the first time they're given.
6. No put-downs.
7. Rinse your plate, glass, and utensils and place them in the dishwasher.
8. Make your bed. (This should become a routine rather quickly.)
9. Knock on the door before entering anyone's room or the bathroom.

Sample Consequences

Match rules with consequences according to the age of your children. Consequences should last no more than one week at a time unless there are serious behavior problems. For children who are three to seven years old, consequences should be for one day at a time. The best consequences are natural. For example, if your teenager parks the car in a "No Parking" zone, the natural consequence is "Cars will be towed and drivers will pay a $75 fine." All consequences can't be natural, but you can make sure they are simple, practical, and meaningful. Some consequences are solely verbal. Your children should know if you are upset with them or disappointed in them. Tell your children that you are unhappy with their behavior. "I'm disappointed in your behavior." "I'm so angry at the way you talked to me." Consequences cause children to feel bad, and you shouldn't be surprised when they're angry at you. Consequences are by necessity uncomfortable and involve deprivation of some reward or exclusion from some privilege or event. Multiple misbehaviors require multiple consequences. Here are some typical consequences:

1. You can't play with your favorite toy.
2. You can't watch television for a day/week.
3. You can't play outside.
4. You can't go out for the weekend.
5. You can't spend the night with a friend.
6. You can't play video games.
7. You can't talk on the telephone or e-mail friends.
8. You can't participate in extracurricular activities at school.
9. You must get up and leave the dinner table and go to your room.
10. If you (your teenager) come in late, you can't go to the next big engagement on the calendar.

Step Four: Teach your child your discipline game plan and repeat the plan often.

The most important part of discipline is the teaching you do. One of the best ways to prevent misbehavior is to repeat the game plan. Each day or each week, go back over the rules and consequences. Talk with your child about the areas where he or she has been getting into the most trouble. Suggest ways to improve. Take advantage of every teaching moment. Make sure that you apply the rules and carry out the consequences every single day without exception. If you're not consistent, how can you expect your child to be? With the passing of time, your children will understand that good behavior is praised and celebrated, and bad behavior is penalized. Most children will accept reasonable consequences because they realize at some level that you are being fair and really are trying to help them grow up.

Many behavior problems are caused by our failure to teach our children on a daily basis that discipline is a normal part of life. Here are the steps to follow in teaching your game plan for discipline:

1. Explain everything to your children. State the obvious and demonstrate your expectations.
2. Practice the game plan with your children. Demonstrate good behavior, good manners, and good conflict resolution skills. Go over all the behaviors that your children keep doing the wrong way.
3. Reinforce rules, consequences, expectations, and understandings. Keep working with your children until your rules become your children's routines.

Step Five: Have family meetings for serious problems that occur over and over again.

I'm not a big fan of weekly family meetings. Busy people don't need one more unnecessary meeting to attend. You can use your family meeting to resolve difficult problems just as a referee at a basketball game calls all the participants over and explains that he won't tolerate any more fighting.

THREE DISCIPLINE GAME PLANS

I have devised three discipline plans that are based on games that many children play or watch: baseball, soccer, and hockey. One positive reason for using discipline plans based on games is that children already have a context. In many cases, your children already know the boundaries and rules for playing baseball, soccer, or hockey. When you transfer basic rules of these games to discipline plans in your family, they are easier for children to understand and to follow. The baseball plan and the hockey plans are the best suited for children ages three to seven. The soccer plan is for children eight to sixteen.

The Baseball Plan

THE BASEBALL PLAN

- For children three to seven.
- Two chances that serve as warnings: "That's one." "That's two."
- 1, 2, 3 strikes, and you're out.
- On strike 3, child receives a consequence for the rest of that day.
- Continued misbehavior produces additional consequences.

This is where knowledge of the basic games that children play will come in handy. For example, I'm a huge baseball fan. I have followed the Atlanta Braves of the National League since 1956. They were still in Milwaukee then. I was a pitcher in high school. In baseball, the most basic rule for a batter is one, two, three strikes, and you're out. Therefore, I use the one-two-three rule in my discipline. My children know that the first strikes are free every day or every week. When a child disobeys a rule before breakfast on Monday morning, I announce, "That's one." Two more and that child will have a consequence. For example, if your child is late for school and that violates one of your family rules about doing things on time, you follow the game plan. Get him or her out of bed, and say, "That's one." On the way out the door, your child growls at you and says some disrespectful stuff. Smile and say, "That's two, because showing respect is a family rule for us." Your children will catch on pretty quickly to the importance of one, two, three and you're out.

Once again, it's important for parents to avoid the trap of micro-parenting. Make sure that you reserve consequences for violation of the four major rules. If consequences pile up before noon and the child has no privileges left for you to take away, you should evaluate your level of strictness. You may need to lighten up a bit.

The purpose of the first two strikes is to give children simple advance warnings as well as opportunities to change their behavior. The baseball plan works best with younger children if consequences last only for a day at a time. Each morning, you should take time to review the previous day's behavior, restore all privileges, and say something such as, "Yesterday you had a hard time remembering and following the rules. I'm sure that you'll do much better today." Use the early morning to teach, repeat the rules, and review behavior patterns. Remind your child about appropriate and inappropriate behaviors.

There are two other crucial parts to the baseball plan. For one thing, you need to have a list of four to six consequences. It's important to listen and observe your children so you can select consequences that actually matter. Parents at my workshops often tell me that taking away privileges has been a waste of time because they took away privileges that really didn't matter to their children.

Remember that your purpose is to get your child's attention and let him or her know that you are serious about discipline.

If your child loses all privileges before noon for three days in a row, you may need to consider shortening the duration of the consequences to four hours at a time, or you may need a new group of consequences. The baseball plan is an evolving plan that will take two or three weeks to refine.

The other important part of the baseball plan is your own consistency. You should make sure that you follow through on the consequences every day for at least four to six weeks. When I question parents at my workshops who have tried and failed at taking away privileges, I learn that failure to be consistent is the biggest factor.

Now, how do you keep score? That is, how do you make sure that both you and your children know exactly where you stand during the week? Keep score of rule violations. You can jot them down in your daily planner. You can put an index card on the refrigerator with your child's name on the card. You can mark each rule violation with a check or a "1." Your child can check on their score. Younger kids should get three strikes on credit a day; older kids three strikes over a week.

The Soccer Plan

THE SOCCER PLAN

- For ages eight to sixteen.
- Keep boundaries and structure.
- Use consistent rules.
- Use yellow card for minor infractions.
- Use red card for major infractions.
- Three yellow cards equal a red card.
- Red card equals suspension of all privileges.

The best and most visual way to help children know where they stand comes from the game of soccer. The soccer field has a definite boundary and structure to it. The game is played by universal rules. If your children play soccer, they are already familiar with its rules and the consequences for breaking them. The referee has yellow cards for minor penalties and red cards for a major misconduct penalty. I suggest that you have three yellow cards for each child. Once a child violates the third rule of the day or week, he gets a yellow card. For each additional misbehavior he gets an additional yellow card. You can make a small pouch or envelope and put it on the refrigerator. Put each child's name on the pouch. The yellow cards are placed in the pouch. The child can always check and see how he's doing. "I would check my pouch if I were you." After receiving three yellow cards, your child's next misbehavior gains him a red card. In soccer, getting a red card means you're thrown out of the game. The child receiving a red card loses all special privileges for the rest of the day for ages three to seven and for the rest of the week for ages seven and up.

You may want to borrow the warnings from the baseball plan. That means your child gets two warnings before receiving the first yellow card. One of the advantages of using the cards is they are a visual reminder. Your child hears you announce the rule violation and he or she sees the yellow or red card. When your child violates a family rule, hand him a yellow card and tell him, "Put this yellow card in your envelope. You won't be about to play outside today."

If you use the soccer plan for children ages three to seven, you can use the yellow cards as warnings, and then use consequences only for the red card. For children eight and older, they should receive a consequence on the first rule violation. They are old enough to understand the connection between behavior and consequences.

For example, your four-year-old has a temper tantrum at the breakfast table. You give her a yellow card to place in your envelope on the refrigerator. Make sure she understands that two more rule violations will mean the suspension of all her important privileges for the rest of the day. An hour later, she hits her younger brother. Since hitting is one of the misbehaviors for which we have zero tolerance, she gets a second yellow card and a period of time to sit in the rocking chair and decide what she will do next time instead of hitting. The time spent in the rocking chair isn't as important as having your daughter tell you her plan for the next time she gets so mad she wants to hit her brother. Also, she needs a reminder that if she violates two more rules today, she will lose all privileges for the rest of the day.

Let's suppose that she gets up from the rocking chair, calls you a nasty name and throws a toy at you. This outburst earns her a third yellow card and the red card. She loses all her privileges for the rest of the day. If she continues to misbehave, you will need to recheck the consequences you're using and change them. You will also need to add additional consequences for the continued misbehavior. Again, the important factor is that you be consistent every day. Discipline is as much an attitude as it is an action.

Children who continue to misbehave in angry and aggressive ways in spite of your consistent application of consequences need a different approach. At this point your child needs help more than he needs more discipline. When the plan fails to change behavior patterns, you should make changes. You can change the consequences. You can change to a new plan. You can use creative discipline.

If your child is a teenager, you can sit down with him, explain the effect of all this conflict on you, and ask him to help you come up with a plan that you can both accept. If one of your older children blows all his privileges by Tuesday, he'll have a rough week. Is there any incentive for him to behave for the rest of the week? Sure. He will have a chance to start over on Sunday. You will need to suffer through the week with your child. On Sunday you can rehearse the plan, repeat the rules, and discuss the problem behavior area with your child. Be positive and say, "I'm confident that you'll have a great week."

The Hockey Plan

THE HOCKEY PLAN

- For younger children ages three to seven.
- Use as a form of time-out.
- Create a "penalty box" space in your home for the violations.
- Assign two to five minutes as cool-down period.
- What will your child do next time?

One last game metaphor may be helpful with small children. In hockey, when a player receives a penalty, he's sent to the penalty box. If you have trouble getting your child to stay in the time-out space, try changing the name to the "penalty box." You can create an enclosed area where your child can't crawl, climb out, or walk away without your help. I know some parents, big hockey fans, who made a penalty box in a corner of one room of their home. After a few trips to the penalty box, their four-year-old son would go put on his hockey gear after an infraction and then go sit quietly in the box until his time was completed.

Your Rulebook

I recommend that you keep a notebook that outlines your rules and your penalties. At the end of each day, jot down the discipline moments that you encountered with your children. In particular, note the responses that you made to the misbehavior. Also, please write down any overreaction on your part. Did you lose your temper? Did you scream and yell? Were you consistent? Did you follow your discipline plan? Don't trust your memory.

Over time, you'll adjust your rules and adapt consequences that are more effective. Your rulebook will help keep you focused.

EMOTIONAL TOUGHNESS

On the one hand, as parent we want to help our children relax, have fun, and enjoy being children. On the other hand, it is our job to teach our children responsibility and self-discipline. Parents tend to live at one or the other of these extremes; they're too permissive or too strict. Balance is the key. Delight and discipline are necessary for a well-balanced life. You can be tough and tender.

Being a parent takes a certain mental and emotional toughness. I really struggle on this point. I spent a lot of time in my early parenting years worrying about how my children felt. I worried when I said "NO!" I worried when I couldn't meet their expectations, requests, and demands. I worried about whether they would still love me when I disciplined them. My own parenting insecurity made it almost impossible for me to make good decisions. In my head, I would know the right decision to make, and then, in the crunch time, I would do the opposite of what I knew was right. This behavior has driven my wife crazy for years. Changing this behavior is no easy task. You can, however, change.

Emotional toughness doesn't mean acting in rude, crude, and offensive ways. Emotional toughness means playing fair. A parent has to do what's best and right and have the integrity to take the response of his or her children without blowing his or her cool. Emotional toughness has nothing to do with how you treat children, but everything to do with how you react to the emotional outbursts of your children.

Parents in my workshops complain about the behavior of their children: "My children think they're in charge." "Our children are so demanding." "My child never, never listens to me." "My children fight all the time." "Our children believe the world revolves around them." "Say no to my child and watch for nuclear temper tantrums." The result? "We walk on eggshells at home to prevent bad behavior." "I lost it." "You won't believe what I said to my kid."

The truth about such complaints is that all children behave this way, and all parents go through the experience. As Bill Cosby puts it in *Fatherhood,* "No matter how calmly you try to referee, parenting will eventually produce bizarre behavior, and I'm not talking about the kids."

As parents, we can stand apart from the "heat of the moment" and observe what is happening. If we are emotionally tough, we can learn not to react, but to evaluate and then step in to make changes and improvements. We can take deep breaths and learn to eliminate ineffective ways of treating children. Learn to use creative discipline. The gift of awareness is a good starting point. Learn to engage in imagined interactions in advance. Remember that you're in charge and you have the power to take positive action. Before you act impulsively and strike out without thinking, take a few moments to move in a more positive direction.

Create an emotional space for yourself. Distance yourself from all your conflicting emotions and your child's misbehavior. Realize that you're capable of handling this particular disruption. Listen to your "inner voice" or your parental intuition. You need creativity. And you need the resolve to take real action.

LIVING IN HARMONY:
PREVENTIVE DISCIPLINE

There are two keys to preventing too many discipline moments in your family's life. The first, as I've emphasized, is the establishment of routines. The second is the formation of a warm, caring, secure home climate. The following principles are designed to remind parents of how essential it is to live with dignity and respect.

- Live together in harmony. Agreement, adaptation, accord, unity, consistency, order, symmetry, and proportion are a few of the words that give meaning to harmony. A harmonious family lives on the same page.
- Live together in love as though you had only one mind and one spirit among you.
- Never act from motives of rivalry or personal vanity, but in humility think more of one another than you do of yourselves. Give your children the benefit of the doubt.
- Help your kids learn to see things from the point of view of other members of the family. Do role-playing: "How do you think Mom feels about that? You pretend to be Mom, and I'll be you."
- Do your work without grumbling or arguing, so that you're well-behaved, sincere, and wholesome. Don't allow laziness to interfere with your performance. Your children will be inspired to follow your example.

- No more temper tantrums or uncontrollable rage, no more nasty thoughts or words about others, no more critical thoughts or words about your family, and no more destructive conversation.

- Don't tell lies. When children tell lies, they violate the basic nature of family life. Lying violates trust, and trust is at the heart of family relationships. Mistrust can disintegrate relationships. So if your child lies to you, the most important step you can take is to treat the matter with the utmost seriousness. Since not telling the truth has such serious ethical consequences, this is one time when your children need a serious lecture or speech from you. Of course, you will want to make sure that you're an excellent model of truth in your own life. Make it clear to your child that you have no toleration at all for lying. Use creative discipline to establish a plan of discipline. You may say, "You've lied to me and that means I can no longer trust you or believe everything you say. For the next two weeks, you'll be required to experience the results of mistrust. I'll be checking to make sure you are telling me the truth. I'm deeply hurt by the fact that you have chosen not to tell the truth, but I'll do everything in my power to help you reestablish trust between us. Remember, we tell the truth in this family."

- Accept life, and be most patient and understanding with one another, always ready to forgive if you have a difference with anyone.

- Don't let bitterness or resentment spoil your home.

- Whatever you do, put your whole heart and soul into it.

- Don't cherish exaggerated ideas of yourself or your importance, but try to have a sane estimate of your capabilities.

- Have a genuine warm affection for one another and a willingness to let others have the credit.

I hope you've gotten my message that a house that practices clear, fair discipline isn't cold or rigid but a home that fosters love and security and sets the stage for children to grow into responsible adults.

CHAPTER 10

ENCOURAGING PARENTING LESSONS I'VE LEARNED FROM EXPERIENCE

IF YOU COULD MAGICALLY GO BACK IN TIME to start over as a parent of small children what would you do differently? Having learned most of what I know about parenting in the school of experience, here are the lessons I want to pass along. You've heard them before in this book, but the lessons have to be repeated. Here's my valedictory address.

The Lessons Have to Be Repeated

By the way, did I tell you that the lessons have to be repeated? Children don't get the point or understand the lesson simply because their parent tells them one time. So cut them some slack and realize that kids will be kids. They're almost never trying to be mean or bad or outrageous. They just don't get the point yet. So repeat the lessons and do so with patience and kindness and gentleness. An article in *USA Today* indicates that young honeybees have to be trained to search for food. Research shows that the young bees take from one to eighteen practice flights before becoming part of the foraging party. Give your kids plenty of practice before they fly. I offer to you the lessons that had to be repeated many times in my home.

Screaming and yelling is ineffective.

A movie advertisement caught my eye: *"SCREAMERS."* "Look," I cried to Johnelle, "a movie about parenting!" Actually the movie was a science-fiction flick. Doesn't parenting sometimes resemble science fiction or a horror story? Children have a knack for stepping on our last nerve. Before we realize it, the decibel level at home registers on the seismograph at the local university. All that screaming creates chaos. Screaming is a bad habit that needs a new address. Children are immune to our shouts. So find another way to get your point across. Screaming at children is a colossal waste of time and energy. Many parents start whispering when their kids start screaming and find that their kids instinctively lower their voices to hear.

Lectures are unproductive and boring.

It's a situation all parents face. A child has a problem, and instead of allowing him or her to solve it, you pour forth a fountain of advice and direction. For example, your son is stuck in time-out. You are ranting, "How many times do I have to tell you not to hit your sister? That's not right! If you hadn't hit her, you wouldn't be in time-out. You could be outside playing with your friends. But no, you had to go and smack your sister. You cause me nothing but grief. What am I going to do with you? I never treated my mother like this. And I never hit anybody in my life either. Why, when I was a little girl…" My mother once told me when I ate too much at dinner, "Rodney, if you hadn't eaten seven baked sweet potatoes, you wouldn't be sick."

Lectures produce the glazed look of a bored audience. Our children are standing before us in body only. Their minds have left the building. Why? You're giving them old information. Your son already knows why he's stuck in time-out. I knew why I had an upset stomach. There's no information. More important, children who have problems don't need instruction, advice, or history lessons. The next time you find yourself wagging your finger in the face of your child, realize you're engaging in a fruitless mission. I know lecturing often feels good, especially if you believe your children are really asking for it. Take a few deep breaths and find ways to promote your child's ability to solve problems rather than babbling on in redundancy.

Your job is to empower your children to solve their own problems. When you tell your child what to do in a nagging, lecturing tone of voice, you invite him to battle—especially if he is a teenager. Instead of lecturing, give your children chances to solve their own problems.

Don't berate your children's best efforts.

Our son Kirkland, after much "parental support," turned in a project for International Day to his third-grade teacher. Ireland was his country of choice for the research project. He dressed as a leprechaun and brought along as many Irish symbols and visual aids as possible. When Johnelle picked him up from school, she discovered that he had gotten a B on the project. She was privately disappointed; wasn't his an A+ effort? With as much tact as possible, she asked, "Kirkland, what do you think Mr. Genco wanted you to do for an A on the project?" Kirkland looked at her as if she were the world's least intelligent person, and said, "Mama! Who cares? B's are great!" Kirkland had done his best; he deserved to take pride in his effort, not feel bad that he didn't get an A.

Given the pressure to succeed, to be number one, to compete at the highest levels, I'm not surprised at the high levels of stress in some children. You need to discover a balance. Give your kids a break. Competition isn't the chief virtue in life. Being number one isn't the only valid reason for living. Vince Lombardi was wrong. Winning isn't the only thing. Children have value and worth simply because they are. As Lewis Thomas, in *Late Night Thoughts* says (while listening to Mahler's Ninth), "A human child, one human child anywhere in the world, is the greatest wonder of the universe."

Don't bribe your children.

To bribe a child is an act of desperation. Of course, desperation is a constant companion of many parents. Cookies are proffered to stop crying in the supermarket. Candy is produced to put an end to temper tantrums. Dollars are forked over for good grades. Buying grades or good behavior sounds like begging—a way of negotiating from weakness. "I'll give you whatever you want if you'll just shut up." "If you'll stop crying, Mommy will give you a whole bag of cookies."

A two-year-old child recognizes and grasps power handed to her by a bribing, defeated parent. Kids will pull your string as long as you let them. A mom at one of my parenting workshops told me, "My two-year-old son is in charge at my house." She had forgotten a basic parenting principle: Never bribe or negotiate with terrorists or toddlers. One will bomb you; the other will drive you crazy.

I agree with Lewis Thomas's assertion that altruism is in our genes. Why? Because when parents bribe children for goodness's sake, they're suggesting that children aren't really good. The end result is that children grow up expecting to be paid for goodness. If, however, altruism is in our genes, we have something to build on. We can teach our children to do good because goodness is good to do, and because they're born to be good.

Don't argue with your children.

Never argue with children is one of my basic rules. There is a difference between a rational discussion and an argument. Argument usually degenerates into excessive displays of emotion along with verbal abuse, sarcasm, and put-downs. Argument, by nature, is confrontational. It suggests winners and losers. Think of the words we use to describe arguing: attack, defend, defeat, and strategy. That's why argument degenerates into verbal warfare. The family loses when you argue with your children.

As an adult, you have a greater responsibility to be reasonable, logical, and mature when your children are being unreasonable, irrational, and immature. Remember, it takes two people to have an argument. You have a choice. You can choose not to argue.

Your children probably take a perverse sense of delight in arguing. They don't even care what they're saying. I call the mindless arguing of my children "yammering." If you argue back, your children will drag you into the quicksand of emotional insanity. Before you know what's happening, you will be arguing, then threatening and screaming. And you will lose. Never argue with children.

If you find yourself slipping into an argument, hit your emotional reset button. Take a deep breath and return to a calm explanation. Here are some ways to avoid arguing:

- "I understand how you feel, but we have decided that you aren't old enough to go to Florida on spring break without adult supervision."
- "I know you're really angry at me, but I have nothing further to add to this conversation."
- "Please give me a few minutes of silence to think about your request."
- "Let me check with your mother. We'll get back to you

tomorrow." (I have a great advantage—Johnelle is a middle school principal. Sometimes I'll say, "Let's check with the principal.")

Make sure you teach everything that you believe to your children.

Bombarded with multiplicity of confusing truth claims, your children need the steady, daily teaching that only you can effectively provide. When you have an uncluttered moment, fill it with good teaching. As your children's primary teachers, you want to give them the skills they need to solve problems, think critically, and creatively, get along with other people, become independent, and live successfully. Even when your children appear bored and determined not to learn, stay the course. There is so much to teach and so little time.

Don't expect a lot of gratitude or understanding. Prepare yourself for waves of criticism, indifference, and complaining. Even teenagers can be like one first-grader a principal told me about. The young man got up from his chair at noon on the first day of school, put on his coat, and headed for the door. The teacher stopped him and asked him, "Where are you going?" "I'm going home," came the first grader's reply. As a kindergarten student the previous year, he had only gone to school for half a day. So he thought it was time to go home. He made a dash for the door and got away from the teacher. Running through the hall, he bumped right into the principal. The principal carefully explained to her runaway student that he'd be staying in school all day, every day. A convinced but unbowed student finally queried the principal, "I just want to know one thing. Who in the hell signed me up for this?" As a parent, you should wade through the resistance to learning thrown up by your children. Teach them everything you value.

There's no reason to tolerate a messy house.

You probably think I'm harping on this point, but I truly believe that a messy house gets a family out of the daily routines that give life meaning and purpose. No, your house doesn't have to be immaculate. But if you spend a few minutes every morning or evening putting things back where they belong, you'll have a smoother life. You'll be more relaxed and there will be less stress.

Teach your children how to keep their rooms reasonably clean. Don't expect miracles. If one of your children has trouble keeping his or her room clean, you can go in each evening and help him or her for a few minutes. "I know you don't like picking up your stuff, but we need to clear the deck before bedtime. Come on, I'll help you." For example, one of our sons kept his room clean and organized to the hilt. His brother, on the other hand, could have cared less. Johnelle asked him, "Wouldn't you like to keep your room clean?" He replied, "No. As long as I can get from the door to my bed, I'm happy." Instead of arguing, lecturing, or punishing, Johnelle simply spent a few minutes each evening helping him pick up his stuff. After a couple of months, she no longer needed to give him any help. He realized it was more relaxing to be in a neater room and he could get it that way in just a few minutes.

It's not necessary to pretend that you have it all together.

No one has all the answers. Even when our answers aren't exactly right, we're still in charge. I don't believe in having it all together. Life is unfinished business all the way. There are surprises, and as a parent you'll have to improvise. Decisions will have to be made on the run. Just when we figure out how to live, someone says it's time to go. Now that my children are grown, I have a clearer understanding of parenting. Your kids don't need to think you're perfect, only that you're human.

People who think they have it all together are under a lot of stress trying to hold it all together. I prefer some spontaneity, surprises, and serendipity. After all, relaxation is preferable to perfectionism.

Don't spend your life at the office.

The office is easier than parenting. You can send me to the office seven days a week and leave me there for sixteen hours a day, and that will be easier than staying at home with three small children for one morning. There is too much life, however, beyond the office to allow ourselves to hide there or get stuck there. You can leave work at the office, and it will be there for you when you return. So go to the office each morning on time. Work hard there. Do your best there. But don't live there. Parents often say, "My family is first in my life." In reality, family often comes in fourth or fifth with work being number one. Your children are waiting at home. Go there often. Stay there as much as possible. Your children need you more than the office does.

I have a few words for dads about the tension between work and family—*more is better.* Spend more time with your children. Show more affection. Enjoy your children more. Love your wife more. While no one gives promotions for being a great dad, the rewards you receive, the emotional satisfaction, and the good that you accomplish will last forever.

Tell stories and work hard to become the best possible storyteller.

Stories are the stuff of life. A great Jewish rabbi once said, "God loves stories; that's why he made us." The really good stories are the ones that last—the ones you can tell over and over again. You know you have a great story when your children plead, "Tell us that story again, Daddy." So go ahead and tell lots of stories.

As I've emphasized, one of the best ways for you to connect with your children is to tell plenty of stories. Through stories communities are formed, intimacies are increased, and connections are made that last forever. Stories define who we are as people. Stories ground us in the daily experience of life. Stories are essential to our well being. As Frederick Buechner says in *Secrets,* "Maybe nothing is more important than that we keep track, you and I, of these stories of who we are and where we have come from and the people we have met along the way because it is precisely through these stories in all their particularity...that God makes himself known to each of us most powerfully and personally."

Be the best possible storyteller. Don't waste a single moment. Fill the air with stories. As Lucy Marsden, in *Oldest Living Confederate Widow Tells All,* puts it:

And young as you are compared to me, you better get your stories in order, child. Because a person's life, it's just about a week. You're getting dressed for school on Monday morning, Momma's two rooms off calling, "You'll be late again, sister, and no written excuse from home this go-round, Miss Molasses in January," and by the time you try and put your foot through your pantaloon's other leg hole, you find it hard to straighten up because you're a woman of eighty-odd and your spine, why it's rusting already. Here you are, Momma long gone, no hope of another note of excuse ever again, and you're still stepping into schoolgirl britches so out-of-date they look plain silly, even to you. You perk and find yourself alone because, hey, it's late on Thursday and I mean your only Thursday, ever, child. Now, for me it's about Sunday evening—late. Always did despise Monday mornings. So just cover your wristwatch till you hear Mrs. Lucy croak, "The End."

Make sure your children learn dignity and respect for all people.

In a world of hate groups and growing intolerance as well as the loss of civility, never teach your children bigotry, prejudice, or racism. Bigots live in their own little world. They keep drawing smaller circles to exclude folks different from themselves. Help your children understand that different is not bad but good. There is only one family and that is the human one. As Emerson put it: "Not until the sun excludes you do I exclude you."

Try not to wallow in guilt over your children's mistakes and failures.

The journey that moves your children from dependence to independence can be littered with bad judgments, bad calls, and big failures on their part. There are lessons we all learn the hard way. Do your best raising your children, but please know that these strong, assertive, and stubborn children are going to make mistakes. When that happens, allow them to face the music and give them additional chances. But don't wallow in guilt over their mistakes.

Grieve for the pain of your children. Help bear their heavy loads, but don't take on guilt as a managing partner. Harry Crews, in the short story "Fathers, Sons, Blood," talks about the universal parental experience of trying to shield our kids from life's body blows. Who among us hasn't tried to keep our children from painful experiences, even when we intuitively know that those experiences will teach them so much and give them an opportunity to prove their resilience? In his short story, Crews relates the exasperation of a father whose son is preparing to drop out of college to pursue a career in music; the father is convinced the son is throwing his life away:

> "Byron, do you know how many boys there are in this country with guitars who think they're going to make a living picking?"
>
> He only smiled and asked, "Dad, when you were my age, how many boys do you think there were in this country who owned typewriters who thought they were going to make a living writing?"

Crews's point is that we have to let our children live out their own dreams, not force them into lockstep with ours, even if it means exposing them to failure. We just need to swallow hard and send them out with encouragement. If they fail, we comfort them and compliment them on the courage to try.

Remember to go out once a week without the children.

You need a break from your kids to renew yourself and your marriage. Don't take children to restaurants before they're ready. Small children and great restaurants don't make good partners. I'm sure you've seen those signs on the front door of restaurants: "No shirts, no shoes, no service." I suggest adding: "No children." Small children aren't ready for prime restaurant time. If you have to take children out to eat, please go to McDonald's. They provide a play area and a "Happy Meal."

For me, a happy meal is a quiet French restaurant in a lovely white board cottage, a glass of wine, soft music, stimulating conversation, and great south Louisiana cuisine and a romantic evening with my wife. Go on and pay the baby-sitter.

You deserve and need the break. If you are a single parent, you need to do something once a week with other adults that remind you that you're a good person. You need to get away from the stress and exhaustion of twenty-four hours a day of total diligence. You've earned some good times.

Always maintain your sense of wonder.

Remember that life as it is given is good. Even when life throws you a curve, the potential for goodness is still present. Watch hummingbirds fly backward as you take a walk in the park with your children. Watch spiders weave webs. Make a list of the seven modern wonders of the world and tell your children about your choices. Stay young as long as possible. Play kids' games. Lose at the games kids play just for the fun of it. Laugh a lot. Learn as much as possible. Share everything you learn. Keep the flames of love alive. Encourage children every moment of every day. And may you be encouraged in the parenting experience, because it's one of life's greater journeys.

CHAPTER 11

BECOMING AN ENCOURAGING PARENT:

THANKS FOR DOING A GREAT JOB

FOR THE PAST FIVE YEARS, I have listened to the voices of thousands and thousands of parents. I have learned that all of them are much better parents than they realize. I want to offer a hearty round of applause for the hundreds of encouraging actions that parents take every day. With hearts filled with love, parents dream for their children, pray for them, desire the best for them, worry about them, and work hard to help them. I'm convinced, from interviews with thousands of parents, that parents need to remember all the wonderful things they do for their children instead of obsessing about the tough discipline moments. After all, there is so much more to parenting than making children behave.

Here is my ode to encouraging parents everywhere. You have my thanks for the marvelous job you're doing. Here's my Top Twenty list of to-be-applauded parenting practices.

1. Thanks for investing in your child's emotional and spiritual life. Steven Covey, business consultant and best-selling author, adapted his winning formula of the seven habits for his family life. He talks a lot about making deposits in the emotional bank account. Let's talk about emotions, especially the emotions of children. First of all, the emotions of children are exaggerated. They tend to be really up or really down; children's behavior is often off the charts. Parents who respond with their own brand of emotional firestorm don't help children grow emotionally. Children catch emotional reactions from their parents. What are the positive emotions we want to share with our children? Happiness, joy, pleasure, excitement, peace, and satisfaction. Teach your children how to handle negative emotions.

2. Thanks for being strong enough to handle the tough times, and being your child's mentor, not his or her best friend. There is a big difference between being a mentor and being a friend. A mentor has serious responsibilities to teach his pupil. The mentor has to have the courage to teach painful lessons. The mentor is not willing to overlook mistakes, faults, or bad decisions. That's the job of a good friend. A mentor's goal is to prepare the pupil for a life of responsibility. Mentors are at times tender and at other times tough. Mentors will criticize, evaluate, motivate, encourage, and push their pupils to succeed. There is a distance between mentors and pupils that doesn't exist between friends. Parents are mentors with lessons to teach their children. To be less is to deprive our children of guidance and wisdom. Remember, your child will make his own friends. Parents with no structures or routines are usually trying hard to be a best friend instead of a mentor. I know a mom with three teenage children who provides them and all their friends with food and drink after school every day. She lets everyone stay as long as they want. Kids are often hanging around at the house at one in the morning on Tuesday or Wednesday. She hangs out with the kids. For some reason, this parent is going through another extended period of adolescence. These kids need a firm, guiding adult, not another friend.

3. Thanks for giving your children boundaries and structures. Parents have to invest time and energy in establishing boundaries and structures for everyday life in the home. Consistency is the key principle.

4. Thanks for always insisting on high expectations. Dreams, hopes, aspirations, desires, goals, and ideas often need a little push. Raising the bar without pushing the child to the extreme is the delicate balancing act that parents have to perform every day.

5. Thanks for talking to and with your children. Talk is the foundation of literacy. Talk is what makes us human. You can do a lot to help prepare your child for good relationships by talking with him on a regular basis. Teach your children to revere the high art of fine conversation.

6. Thanks for listening to your children. The power of empathy is so crucial. As a parent you have three sets of ears: your biological ears, your eyes, and your heart. We will hear with our ears, but unless we use eyes and heart, we're not really listening. Trust your inner voice. Don't wait for proof. A Cosby rerun I watched recently revolved around Mom believing in her heart that something was going on with Theo. She didn't have any evidence. She lacked proof. All she had to go on was her intuition. Guess what? Mom turned out to be right! She held a mock family court and got to the bottom of the problem in a humorous and nonthreatening way.

7. Thanks for spending time with your children. Don't make the mistake of taking the relationship for granted. Parents have to spend time with children in order to give the relationship a chance to grow in positive and healthy ways. Never assume that children know how much they're loved. This doesn't mean that children need parents to be with them every moment of every day. Recent surveys indicate that children believe their parents spend enough time with them.

8. Use your imagination to paint a positive picture of the world for your child. Parents are in charge of the home climate. You can create a socially toxic environment if you're constantly complaining.

You will teach your children cynicism, despair, and pessimism if you're always down on life. I'm not suggesting that you lie to children or teach them "pie in the sky by and by" philosophy. But you're the artist who imprints the meaning of life on the souls of your children. Let your painting be for goodness and beauty.

9. Thanks for challenging your children to grow emotionally, physically, spiritually, and intellectually. Robert Frost suggests that people who live at the foot of a mountain are unlikely to ever attempt climbing the mountain. Go ahead and give your children mountains to climb. Never settle for mediocrity.

10. Thanks for working on projects together as a family. The key issue isn't whether Mom works outside the home, but whether the family spends time together after work and school. Children left to themselves will have great difficulty taking the right road or making good decisions or learning good study habits or succeeding in life. Children are not adults and therefore they need adult guidance. This guidance has to be constant and consistent. Parenting is an exhausting job.

11. Thanks for playing physical, outdoor games with your children. The purpose here isn't winning but spending time having fun together. Never forget that childhood is designed to be fun.

12. Thanks for teaching your children conversational skills. In talking with your child, ask open-ended, specific questions. In other words, narrow the scope of your questions. If you ask a child, "How was the picnic?" you will probably only get "It was OK" in return. Ask him what in particular he liked best about the school picnic. Encourage him to give you real examples. And please stop asking your child, "How was your day?" and accepting "Fine" for an answer. Your child has a plethora of daily experiences. Ask more specific questions. "What did you do when you first got to school today?" "Who did you play with at recess?"

13. Thanks for teaching your children social skills. I know one powerful reason for teaching social skills. You will save your child a lot of potential embarrassment in later life. Garth Brooks sings, "I'm not much on social graces, but I've got friends in low places." I would rather my children be socially capable of handling any situation. At least once each month have a family meal in the dining room (you usually save that room for strangers—what a waste). Use all your best china, silver, and crystal. While enjoying a marvelous meal, demonstrate good table manners and help your children learn how to act at a grown-up party. Don't forget to thank the chef: "Darling, you're a marvelous cook!" My second suggestion is to let your children take part in your adult parties. They don't need to stay for the whole evening, but they do need to experience the social excitement of parties.

14. Thank you for teaching your children values that are universal to all cultures. There are lifeskills that children need to assimilate into their developing character: integrity, honesty, responsibility, empathy, compassion, and understanding.

15. Thanks for encouraging your children's lifelong learning. One of the privileges of parenting is to share with your children the joy of lifelong learning. Every day encourage your children to explain their thinking aloud. This will help them understand more clearly the ideas they're expressing. Ask your children probing questions. Expect them to find solutions to problems.

16. Thanks for helping your kids mature by delegating the chores. As a parent, you have awesome delegating powers. Here's a way to make some time for yourself. Instead of caving in to the stress of doing everything, make a list of all the tasks you're now doing around the house. Wow! That's one huge list. Now, if you really want to save some time, start a new column next to all those exhausting tasks. Write down the name of a child who can do each task. You will experience so much relief as you pass along dozens of tasks to your children. While the kids won't do the jobs as well or as quickly, the good news is powerful—you're not staying up late to complete all those household chores. Go ahead and start a new trend at your house. I bet you're a born one-minute manager. Don't try to do everything by two P.M. on Tuesday.

17. Thanks for reading out loud to your children. As soon as possible, allow your children to read out loud to you. Remember that a child pointing at the pictures in a book and telling a story in his or her own words is reading. By the time your children start to school, they should be reading. Early reading experiences will enhance your children's future academic achievement.

18. Thanks for communicating with notes, cards, and letters. Use every possible form of communication to get the message of unconditional love across to your children.

19. Thanks for using daily forms of verbal encouragement. "Now you have the hang of it." "Fantastic! Terrific!" "Keep up the good work!" "I have never seen anyone do it better." "I knew you could do it." "Keep working on the problem, you're getting better."

20. Thanks for balancing family, work, and social life. Your children will always remember the wonderful times you spent with them.

Remember: When the going gets tough, stop for a moment, take a breath, close your eyes, and remember your beautiful child taking those first few steps. Remember your open arms and your encouraging words. You can be that encouraging parent every day of your life.

ADDITIONAL READING

Calkins, Lucy. *Raising Lifelong Learners: A Parent's Guide* (Addison-Wesley, 1997). Specific help for parents in helping children read, write, study, and learn. There's a wealth of material that parents will be able to use in motivating learning.

Coloroso, Barbara. *Kids Are Worth It!* (Avon Books, 1994). Here's a parenting book about meeting kids' needs and working with them to make decisions and solve problems. Based on the classic work of Haim Ginott. Excellent how-to book for parents.,

Johnson, Louanne. *School Is Not a Four-letter Word* (Hyperion, 1997). The techniques of good teachers can be helpful for parents. Encouragement for parents who are struggling to keep their children interested in school.

Pollack, William. *Real Boys* (Henry Holt and Company, 1998). Parents raising boys will want to read this work. At last the myths of boyhood are exposed. Big boys can cry after all, and there's much more about the loneliness and propensity for violence faced by boys in our culture.

Seligman, Martin E. P. *The Optimistic Child* (Harper Perennial, 1996). A proven program for helping children learn resiliency and conflict resolution skills. This is my favorite book for parents.

INDEX